The GARDEN LOG

By-the-Month GARDENING

What to Do and When

by
Jean Skeath Stahl

Jean Skeath Stahl

Illustrations by Jean Skeath Stahl

The GARDEN LOG
By-the-Month
GARDENING
What to Do and When

Visit the author's Website: www.thegardenlog.com

Jean Skeath Stahl
P.O.Box 500, Tylersport, PA 18971
(jrstahl@erols.com)

Printed in the United States of America

Stahl, Jean Skeath
The GARDEN LOG, By-the-Month Gardening, What to Do and When.
Cover Photo: A meadow of tulips in Harleysville, Pennsylvania, taken by Christina R. Forbes.
Author Photo by Bob Esposito, courtesy of The Hearthstone Town and Country Newspaper.

Second Printing

ISBN: 0-9715375-0-X

Table of Contents

January

February

March

April

May

June

July

August

September

October

November

December

Introduction

I often meet gardeners at social gatherings and meetings. Someone will mention that they missed a certain newspaper column of mine and would like to review the information it contained. They say it can be mind-boggling when one is not sure how and when to do certain things, such as fertilizing, planting at the best times, pruning, or starting bulbs for indoor forcing. I have been asked why some seedlings fall over and play dead. A gentleman lamented that his tomato plants ended up lifeless last year, just at the time he should have been enjoying a harvest. I agree that to the occasional gardener, failures can be devastating. Everyone's gardening expectations naturally run high, including my own, and when something goes wrong, it can be very discouraging.

Therein lies the reason for this publication -- to offer a refresher course with information at your fingertips for many kinds of gardening activities, plus a month-by-month list of tasks that help the gardener know what tasks should be taken care of at certain times. It is my hope that this book, based on my newly-revised newspaper columns of 12 years, will help make your own efforts more fun and successful and bring you more self-confidence in how you handle your gardens.

All of my growing suggestions and solutions are related to the Plant Hardiness Zone 6, which is explained in the book's February section.

Zone 6 encompasses a diagonal path of geography, roughly, from eastern Massachusetts, through eastern and central Pennsylvania, zig-zags by topography through all of Kentucky to New Mexico. Then it squiggles north-westward through the Rockies to Washington state.

Long ago, it was obvious to botanists that plants that grew happily in Maine just didn't make it in Georgia, and vice versa. The U. S. Department of Agriculture broke down the whole of the United States into growing zones with tropical plants being found in Zones 10 and 11 in southern Florida, and alpine ones flourishing far north in Zone 2 in Maine, and Zone 1 in Canada.

Plant Hardiness Zones overlap somewhat, since elevation and exposure play a part in early or late frosts. The Zone map is only a guide, but years of experience will reveal all the overlaps that lie within your own garden.

Many plants that are described in catalogs and that are available at garden centers are usually suitable for a wide range of Zones, so you will find, in reading this book, that many specific plants mentioned can be quite durable in a neighboring Zone.

There are very good reasons for doing home gardening besides just liking to get back to Nature. In times of economic stress, it can provide food for the table, both in fresh and preserved forms. It also acts as emotional therapy, providing the physical effort of productive activity while releasing the mind of some of its burdens.

For whatever reasons you may garden, and whatever plants you choose to call your own, may they and you, through this guidebook, be happy, healthy and may you find sheer enjoyment.

Jean Stahl

Acknowlegements

I extend my special thanks to...

...Ray, who was supportive through it all,
...Rod and Wendy Wood, publishers of The Hearthstone Town and Country Newspaper, Red Hill, PA, who had faith in me,
...Julie Marlin, my friend and mentor, Anne Woodbury, my friend and cheer leader, and John Kevin, Jr., who always had answers to my questions,
...Christina R. Forbes, my photographer,
...Robin L. Forbes and Bonny Jean Forbes, my computer and website gurus,
...Mary Concklin, County Agent and all the ladies in the office of Penn State Extension Service, Montgomery County, whose patience I must have worn thin,
...Lorraine Shisler of Shelly Farm and Home Center, Lois Wismer of The Herb Shed, Kevin Crilly of the Green Lane Nature Center, Elizabeth Botti, Nancy and Don Roan for information and insights when I needed them.

January
Checklist

✔ Garden markers can be created out of bleach bottles after cutting off tops and bottoms with large scissors. Use a permanent magic marker to prevent fading or washing off.

✔ Are there pet fish in your house? If so, when cleaning the fishbowl, save the old water. It is rich in nitrogen and is great to use for watering indoor foliage plants.

✔ Employ your unused watering can by unscrewing the sprinkler cap and storing aside. Put birdseed into the can and use it to pour seed into bird feeders.

✔ Over watering kills more house plants than non-watering does. Test the soil surface with your finger first. If it feels dry, it's time to water. If you notice that water collects and stands in the dish beneath the plant, pour it out.

✔ Wood ashes from your fireplace can be sprinkled any time on the lilacs and in the vegetable garden. Berried plants are sweetened in flavor by a light dusting of wood ashes. Use only one application, though. Too much will raise pH and create problems.

✔ If you burn coal in your house do not use coal ashes in the garden. While coal ash could be a good soil conditioner it contains toxic ingredients, such as boron, arsenic, lead and mercury, keep it out of your gardens.

✔ Have you been feeding the birds? Add something new to their diets such as suet or stale doughnuts, or cornmeal mixed with peanut butter. They appreciate fatty foods. When the ground is snow covered their chances of finding wild seeds to eat is slim.

✔ Winter time is planning time for gardeners. Before turning to your seed catalog, take inventory of seeds left over from last summer. Then it's time to start your catalog shopping. (see *Seed Catalog Strategies,* for January.)

✔ As branches come down in winter storms, collect them into a pile nearby. Birds use brush piles as shelter from predators. Strew some seeds into the pile and soon dozens of happy birds will be using it as a refuge.

✔ Push away winter for a little while by bringing in pussy willow branches. Let them soak in water for a few days to swell the buds a bit, but arrange them dry.

✔Use January as your "down time" to visualize this year's garden, landscaping and lawn. In some catalogs the reader may find a page or two with a convenient grid that will help orient how much working space may be in your garden.

✔A friend suggested spraying a sticky snow shovel with a no-stick cooking spray, claiming that it will prevent snow from clinging to the shovel, making the shoveling job much easier. It really works.

✔Start some grapefruit seeds, after soaking them in hot water overnight, and potting them in compost for the window sill. They will sprout and eventually produce glossy, green leaves which are nice for garnishing fruit servings.

✔New Year's Resolutions for the gardener might be:

I resolve not to go outside into a thawed garden with good shoes on.

I resolve to watch the calendar carefully to avoid starting my garden seeds too soon.

I resolve not to go outside to peek at my growing things, forget to come in, and find dinner is scorched.

I also resolve to gather all my sticks for kindling *before* it rains or snows, not after they have become saturated.

Apt for January are William Blake's words:
"In seed time learn, in harvest teach, in winter enjoy."

Is There a Knack to Feeding the Birds?

When there is no snow outside and the landscape looks dismal, that's the best time to enjoy feeding the birds. Well, yes, there are good things about this, and some bad, but that's life. After all, you do have to go out into the cold occasionally to refill the feeders.

When we first started feeding the birds, we picked the cheapest seed available and lugged it home. It was a while before we became more fine-tuned in this exercise. We found that the cheaper mixes draw birds that scoop and scatter the unwanted filler to the ground to seek the occasional sunflower seed that is in the mix. Many of these scattered seeds find their way into gardens where they sprout into a motley assortment of weeds. The accumulated pile on the ground smothers grass and soon begins to rot, drawing ground-feeding birds. The rotted seed is known to cause illness among them. It also draws small rodents such as mice and moles.

There are options to keep wintering birds healthy and visiting your bird buffet regularly without leaving a big mess.

Perch-feeding birds favor oilseed (black oil sunflower). It comes hulled or unhulled. Hulls will end up on the ground. Keep these raked up before they smother grass or draw little rodents. The oilseed is not appetizing to European starling, brown-headed cowbird or English sparrow. That's a big plus. These three species have bad reputations as burglars, thieves and murderers! (See *Bad News Birds*, January.)

Niger (thistle seed), a bit more expensive, brings purple and house finches, gold finches and pine siskins.

Peanut hearts or bits attract blue jays, titmice, red winged blackbirds and chickadees but beware that peanuts also draw starlings, one of the Bad News Birds.

Insect-eating birds enjoy peanut butter mixed with cornmeal or cereal. Special peanut butter feeding stations can be bought or the mixture can be spread onto a pine cone or piece of bark.

Mockingbirds love fruits -- sweet raisins, orange slices, apple bits and even grapes. Orioles and overwintering robins also like pieces of pears.

Suet is the mainstay of woodpeckers, titmice and crows. Wrens will often be seen picking up suet crumbs beneath the suet cages. It is the tastiest and least expensive energy food, especially if mixed with seeds. Try this recipe: 1 cup liquid beef suet, 2 cups seeds and/or fruit pieces, ½ tablespoon sand. Combine and let harden in muffin tins or empty cat food cans. Refrigerate until needed.

Keep a bird identification book near your windows to enjoy looking up every unfamiliar one that shows up for lunch.

Pest Portraits
The Bad News Birds

The European starling is a black bird with white speckles and has a short tail. It was first introduced in New York's Central Park in 1890 and has spread to every part of the continent. It was originally brought here because of its big appetite for harmful insects. This is of great benefit to humans, but the starling also consumes fruit and grain crops. It competes fiercely with native birds for territory and nesting cavities. It is equally at home in farmlands, orchards and even populated areas. Some flocks are known to number in the thousands.

The brown-headed cowbird is the murderer in our world of birds. It will invade other birds' nests, often dumping out eggs to lay their own or adding their own to the eggs already there. The original owners of the nest return to set, only to hatch baby cowbirds. The adult cowbirds fly away as the busy surrogate parents struggle to feed the greedy family of cowbird young.

That cute little English sparrow, or house sparrow, with its brown, stubby little body also has bad habits. This aggressive bird drives others away from nesting areas. It was brought here in 1850. By 1910, being very adaptable, it had established itself in every region of the United states, in the city as well as the country. They originally thrived on horse droppings, finding many seeds in manure. Since the common use of the horse has declined, sparrow numbers have also declined somewhat.

These Bad News Birds actually do better foraging for meals on their own. From their large populations, it would seem they do quite well.

Seed Catalog Strategies

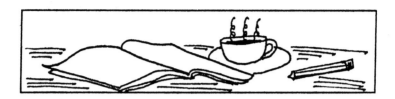

S eed catalogs in my house start stacking up in January. Before doing any catalog shopping, the first task is to take an inventory of old seeds. Last year's parsley, lettuce and corn might still yield some sprouts but chances are slim. Most other seeds are viable for 3 years; musk melon will still germinate after ten years. I've often used garden seeds that were a couple years old and they germinated quite well. Storage in a cool and dry place helps keep them fresh.

You can test the viability of old seeds. Sprinkle about a dozen on a damp paper towel. Fold it over and cover with plastic wrap to retain moisture. Check daily for timely sprouting. If you see sluggish or irregular sprouting, discard the seeds and order new ones.

About those catalogs -- one can feel intimidated by pictures of fruits, flowers and vegetables portrayed in crisp, dewey perfection. Does anyone's garden *really* look this good? Not two gardens are alike in soil type, climate conditions, disease and insect problems, so our own results just might fall a little short of catalog perfection.

Success begins in reading the fine print. It contains a goldmine of information. Find the zone map (see *Plant Hardiness Zones*, February) for your location. Note the number of frost-free days. Find out the number of days to maturity for each variety that interests you. That's the number of days it takes from the day of planting outside to harvest, whether by seed or transplant. By choosing those seeds that have the earliest maturity dates, you may have time for a second crop.

Many plants need full sun (six or more hours a day) in order to do their best. Some varieties do well in shade or part shade and most catalogs indicate this for you.

Other things you will want to know before choosing seeds will be cold sensitivity, drought tolerance, container gardening choices, heirloom types, deer resistance, hummingbird or butterfly attracters, plus cultural facts and recipe suggestions. Some seed companies advise calling a special telephone number that they maintain for help if you experience problems.

How can anyone go wrong with all this assistance? Catalogs become great reference books during the growing season. Discard them only after next year's arrive in the mail box.

What? You Didn't Get Any Catalogs?

We can fix that. Below are a few companies that offer catalogs. After you have become a seasoned catalog recipient, you will notice in magazine ads many other companies to explore.

Most seed companies breed their own varieties and no other company will have that particular one. Explore these new varieties. Often times, they are real winners.

Once you start reading seed catalogs, you may become addicted.

Shepherd's Garden Seeds
30 Irene Street
Torrington, Connecticut 06790
1-860-482-3638
www.shepherdseeds.com

Seeds of Change
P.O.Box 15700
Santa Fe, NM 87506
1-888-762-7333
www.seedsofchange.com

W. Atlee Burpee &Co.
Warminster, PA 18974
1-800-888-1447
website: www.burpee.com

Henry Field's Seed & Nursery
415 N. Burnett
Shenandoah, Iowa 51602
1-800-235-0845
www.henryfields.com

Geo. W. Park Seed Co., Inc.
1 Parkton Avenue
Greenwood, SC 29647
1-800-845-3369
website: www.parkseed.com

Nichols Garden Nursery
1190 N. Pacific Highway
Albany, Oregon 97321
1-541-928-9280
www.pacificharbor.com/nichols/

Johnny's Selected Seeds
Foss Hill Road
Albion, Maine 04910
1-207-437-4301
website: www.johnnyseeds.com

Thompson & Morgan
P.O.Box 1308
Jackson, NJ 08527
1-800-274-7333
www.thompson-morgan.com

Harris Seeds
600 Saginaw Drive
P.O.Box 22960
Rochester, NY 14692
1-800-514-4441
website: www.harrisseeds.com

Gurney's Seed & Nursery
110 Capital Street
Yankton, SD 57079
1-605-665-1671
website: gurneys.com

Some companies are devoted to specialties and are worth a good read:

Vermont Bean Seed Company
Garden Lane
Fair Haven, VT 05743
1-803-663-0217
website: www.vermontbean.com

Totally Tomatoes
P.O.Box 1626
Augusta, GA 30903
1-803-663-0016
website:www.totallytomato.com

Dutch Gardens (all bulbs)
P.O.Box 200, Adelphia, NJ 07710
1-800-818-3861
website:www.dutchgardens.com

Brent and Becky's Bulbs
7463 Heath Trail
Gloucester, VA 23061
1-804-693-3966
www.brentandbeckysbulbs.com

Jackson & Perkins Co. (Roses)
1 Rose Lane
Medford, Oregon 97501
1-800-292-4769
www.jacksonandperkins.com

Roots & Rhizomes (Daylilies, iris, hostas, perennials)
P.O.Box A
Randolph, WI 53956-0118
1-800-374-5035
website: www.rootsrhizomes.com

Arena Rose Company
P.O.Box 3096/525 Pine Street
Paso Robles, CA 93447
1-888-466-7434
www. ArenaRoses.com

These companies specialize in garden tools and supplies. They offer lots of good browsing and many gift-type garden products.

Langenbach
644 Enterprise Avenue
Galesburg, IL 61401
1-800-362-1991
website:www.langenbach.com

Kinsman Company
River Road,
Point Pleasant, PA 18950
1-800-733-4146
www.kinsmangarden.com

Gardener's Supply Company
128 Intervale Road
Burlington, VT 05401
1-800-863-1700
website:www.gardeners.com

Caring for Your Gift Plants

Amaryllis (*Hippeastrum*), a dramatic winter plant, is a favorite at holiday time. Available in so many luscious colors, it is difficult to choose which is the loveliest. They are rarely a disappointment, even though they are nothing but a huge dormant bulb when bought. After a brief wait they come forth into sensational blooms. The care and feeding of an amaryllis is always printed on its box, so will not be repeated here. I suggest that you buy the pre-planted kind that is ready for growing as soon as the box is opened and the bulb watered. Others, which come as a kit and may require special planting instructions, can sometimes be disappointing in results. A non-green-thumber might not appreciate this.

After blooming, cut off the stalks to allow the bulb to store energy. It can be left in its pot to continue growing until the leaves dry. In the fall, repot, and start watering. It may not bloom the second year, but will promise flowers for the next.

Poinsettias (*Euphorbia*) are quite simple to care for. In displaying your poinsettias, the smaller, 6-inch potted ones are great to group into baskets, and place on mantels and window sills on beds of greenery. In other words, use in small spaces. Larger ones display to better advantage on a coffee table, hutch or even on the floor. The very large, hanging baskets will look wonderful wherever they are, as long as their requirements are met.

> "Poinsettias can be mildly poisonous if ingested."

If you receive poinsettias as gifts or have bought them for yourself, a plant care sheet may have been included. If not, the facts are simple.

Remember it is a tropical plant and has been living in a humid greenhouse. It may drop a few leaves but don't panic. It is adjusting to a typical, low-humidity household environment. Just keep the soil moist, not wet, and let it dry a bit between waterings. Keep it in bright light. As with all plants, keep your poinsettia out of cold drafts and away from direct heat of a fireplace or hot air vent. You may and away from direct heat of a fireplace or hot air vent. You may fertilize with a high nitrogen food such as 12-6-6. They are known to bloom for months. Perhaps that is why the ivory-colored, pink, or peach poinsettias are so popular -- they aren't so reminiscent of the red-and-green of Christmas time as March and April come.

It is of some interest to know that poinsettias can be mildly poisonous if ingested. The white sap of this plant can be toxic. It is best that they be kept out of reach of young children and nibbling pets.

Christmas Cactus (*Schlumbergera*) plants are also popular at this time of year and at Thanksgiving time. But the plants called Christmas cactus and Thanksgiving cactus are the same plant. Each is treated by the grower to bloom at a specific time.

As a Christmas gift, this particular one will arrive in bloom and will continue to bloom for a long period. When mild weather comes in the spring, place it outside in dappled sunlight, flowers and all. It should then stop blooming in order to rest and develop new buds for the next round of blossoms.

"This plant is actually a succulent and requires semi-dry soil at all times."

This plant needs a period of dormancy. In October place it in a room of 50 to 55 degrees. Withhold water, supplying only enough to keep it from shriveling. Give it daylight only; no artificial light.

In November, start increasing water a little at a time. You will soon see new growth start. Gradually move it into full sunlight.

This plant is actually a succulent and requires semi-dry soil at all times. Fertilizing can begin now on a schedule of about every two weeks.

My mother's plants bloomed almost constantly in a very cold spare room where she often forgot to water them. Figure out your own method and routine. Whatever works for you is the best method going.

The Trees in Your Yard

Just as with human beings, trees have a lot to offer, but can also have their faults. Certain trees provide shade along polluted highways but you might not want one of those in your yard. Some grow where others won't. Others display beautiful, changing bark colors, but make frequent raking necessary. Keep in mind that there are a large number that grow well in our area but may be considered nuisance trees. If you already own some of these, see if you agree. When shopping for new trees, know what you want. Will you want large ones for shade to reduce summer heat buildup, or to act as a winter windbreak? Do you want privacy screening; a display of decorative foliage, berries or fruits? Do you like smaller ones in groupings for a focal point? See what you think of these that are known as nuisances.

Maples. Silver maple is one of the least desirable trees you could choose. Roots are shallow. Because it is a fast grower, the wood is weak. It bears thousands of seeds, meaning that you will be pulling out lots of maple seedlings. The autumn foliage is pale tan.

The Norway maple was once used as a street tree because of its large, dense crown. It lifts sidewalk blocks and driveway paving, and spreads thousands of seeds in garden beds. It has such an impenetrable root system that it interferes with grass growth and can infiltrate underground household pipes. Leaf color in autumn is bright gold.

Ginkgo, an attractive pyramid type tree, is either male or female. The female sets fruits which have a rancid smelling flesh. Although the nut inside is edible, the repulsive fruits are hardly desirable in the lawn where they will get stepped on and mowed over, venting their obnoxious odor. The males are often used as street landscaping because of their slow growth rate that does not interfere with street wiring and with roots that do not lift paving. Shop carefully if ginkgo is still your choice and select the males only.

Black locust is disease and insect prone and produces seeds prolifically. Clusters of showy spring flowers are its only redeeming feature. Beyond that, do not depend on black locust for a permanent planting. I am told by a friend who has a grove of them that as firewood, black locust has a very high heat value. If you are fortunate enough to also have a grove of them, keep them going for fuel use.

Honey locust sports dangerous thorns; however, thornless varieties are available at nurseries. Honey locust shares lovely blossoms, as well as weak wood, with the black variety. It is a graceful, airy tree. If used as a fireplace fuel, it too has a high heat value.

Horse chestnut. Many thrive in our area and are majestic trees with spreading branches; truly a beauty of a tree visually. However, it should be kept in mind that the fruit of the common variety is poisonous.

Mimosa. Although pretty, pink/red, fragrant flowers bloom all summer, this very dainty tree easily develops webworm infestations and other insect and disease problems. It bears multitudinous seeds which, left to their own devices, sprout easily to crowd out native flora. For this reason it has a reputation as an invasive.

Black walnut produces toxins that are poisonous to many plants. Wherever leaves fall, the soil can become tainted, sometimes enough to make desirable vegetation struggle to survive. Left in a wooded area, its nuts are used by wildlife and can be collected for shelling. Disposal of husks requires care, for they, too, are toxic, producing an indelible stain that can mar paving or be carried by shoes onto a porch or into the house.

Snake Plants as Pets

I never heard anyone say they actually like snake plants (*Sanserviera trifasciata*). In homes they often sit alone and look like orphans. But give them a chance. They are very friendly companions; never temperamental and they never complain. Sometimes they even bloom. They're known by many names -- sanservia, hemp plant and (oh, yes) mother-in-law tongue. Quite unlike mothers-in-law, they thrive on neglect and the only way to kill one is to drown it.

These tough plants can tolerate long periods in dim corners but will do fine in bright light, too. They belong to the succulent family which means the soil does not need a lot of moisture. They can go for as long as a week or two in winter without water. When a mature plant becomes potbound, it will send up stalks of dainty, white, fragrant blossoms. Light fertilizing is necessary only once a month during spring and summer. Now that is not a demanding plant.

But they look so dull, you say? Maybe they do, but all they need is a little attention. One plant standing by itself never won prizes for being interesting, but a grouping creates a focal point on any stair landing or foyer.

To add more interest, choose a larger pot to combine two or more planted to one side, adding a smaller, lower-growing plant on the other side such as ivy geranium, purple heart or a couple of small jade plants. Just be sure that the smaller ones have the same care requirements as the snake plants do.

If you like, a topping of white stones can create impact. Voila. Your snake plant has now become a member of the family, and is looking like it finally belongs.

Of Weeds and Wildflowers
Chickweed

It is often considered a weed. It is like a soft, mossy ground cover that displays tiny, white, star-like flowers. But pretty as it is, it is devilish to get rid of if you don't want in your gardens.

Chickweed (*Stellaria media*) is the plague of many gardeners. Left to itself it forms a pleasant, green matting. Some gardeners use it on paths between stepping stones or in rock gardens. Problem is, it creeps way beyond where one would like it to be. Prolific, it can reseed itself up to five times in a season. It endures the winter, almost to the point of being evergreen, and even puts on a little growth spurt when winter temperatures fluctuate as with a January thaw.

If you do not want in in your gardens, do not feel guilty about pulling it up. When the soil is soft you will notice the roots are fibrous and spreading. Chances are that another little crop of seeds has already been produced. Persist in removing it before those winking star-like flowers become seed pods.

One way to reduce its hold in your garden beds is by using mulch. (see *Removing the Mystery of Mulch*, April). It will save you a lot of work.

Chickweed can have its merits. It is actually edible. Its leaves can be boiled for a minute or two and served as spinach would be, or used fresh in salads. It offers sustenance to wildwife during the winter since it stays green and even continues to bloom.

The lowly chickweed has many pros and cons to its existence. If and when it appears in your private Eden, you may choose for yourself whether it is an asset or liability.

herb of the Month
Chives

G arden chives (*Allium schoenoprasum*) is one of those plants that can grow faithfully as a perennial in the mild months and yet willingly serve as a houseplant for the winter. Its sweet, mild onion flavor can enhance many recipes.

The clump of chives in your garden consists of clustered bulbs, each producing strands of tubular leaves in a healthy green color for cutting all summer long. In the early summer, chives produce flower stalks that support pretty, lavender blossoms. Edible, they too are excellent garnishes in soups or salads. The blossoms taste mildly of onion, just like its green leaves (see *Stop and Eat the Flowers*, July).

To bring in for the winter, simply slice down through a clump with a trowel and remove a section for potting. This can be done in September. Once lifted out of the ground, trim the longest of the roots and pot with compost and garden soil. The empty space left in the soil should be filled back in and tamped down. Leave the potted chives outdoors until after frost has caused the tops to die back. During this time the roots in the pots are becoming established. Then bring them inside, put in a bright spot, keep soil moist but not wet, and watch the new leaves sprout that will flavor recipes.

When I was still a beginning gardener, a friend offered me a subdivision of her chives, with instructions how to plant and grow it. It was probably the first plant I was ever given and it encouraged me to feel that I might have a green thumb after all. Chives have the happy faculty of growing well in almost any garden.

When keeping them as houseplants keep in mind that they do require about five or more hours of sun a day. If your window does not receive this much sun, they will languish. An solution is to use a fluorescent lights suspended about 8 inches above the plant and left on for 12 to 15 hours a day. Temperatures are not a problem for chives. Seventy degrees is adequate for daytime and about 60 degrees for night. Most homes provide these agreeable temperatures.

Rainy Day Quiz

Wintertime represents a lull in the gardening cycle that we enjoy while freezing temperatures outside induce dormancy in many of our plants. For ourselves, we do not really like to become couch potatoes, but succumb to it for a refreshing pause after the activity of holidays.   For many plants and bulbs this winter period of darkness and low temperatures prepares them for great performances in the spring. This cycle is part of the grand scheme that Nature provides.

Meanwhile, here is a little fun for you. Explore your knowledge of houseplants by answering true or false to these questions.

1. More plants perish from over watering than under watering.
2. House plants benefit from winter fertilizing.
3. I can safely save my old clay flower pots for future reuse.
4. There is no difference between a plastic pot and clay pot as a plant container.
5. Misting humidity-loving plants is best done late in the day.
6. Once my amaryllis bulb is spent, I must throw it away.
7. Nibbling or teething on certain house plants is good for my pet cat.

Answers to Quiz

1. True. Excessively wet soil presses oxygen out of the soil around the roots, making them unable to support leaves. The probable result is leaf drop and can cause the plant to die.
2. False. Most house plants benefit from light feeding, but only during their active growth period -- spring and summer. During the normal resting stage, withhold fertilizer.
3. True. But you may want to take some precautions. Clay pots should be treated to kill off harmful organisms. In a bucket or sink, soak empty pots in a solution of 9 parts water and one part bleach to kill fungus

diseases, molds or any other organisms that were left over from previous use. Rinse well and allow to dry.

4. False. Some experts say there is no difference, but I disagree. It is too easy to over water a plastic-potted plant because plastic does not permit respiration through the sides. Soil that may feel dry to the touch on top may still be wet at the bottom. On the other hand, clay dries out much faster, which means more frequent checking.

5. False. Mist your plants in the morning so plants will have time to dry off and not stand damp overnight. You do not want to create an atmosphere for mold or fungus problems.

6. False. With patience, bulbs can be brought into bloom again. They can spend the summer outdoors and be brought inside in the early fall for repotting and new growth.

7. False. Protect Tabby from poisonous plants if she/he is a nibbler. Chrysanthemums, ivies, poinsettia, diffenbachia, philodendrons, and daffodils are culprits.

January Note: Keep window sill plants away from the glass by about 20 inches, if possible. In extremely cold weather, plant tips or leaves risk being frosted if lying against cold glass.

Tomatoes in January?

Not from the grocery store, thank you, but from seed catalogs. I've made my selections already and will probably overbuy. In my enthusiasm, I always do.

There is just one point regarding tomato seed -- or tomato plant -- selection that will make a difference to you in the garden, come July. You will want to make the right choice.

Perchance you have come across the words determinate and indeterminate when reading up on tomato seeds/plants in catalogs.

Determinate varieties are usually bush plants that do not need to be staked since they are rarely larger than about three feet. The determinate type will set fruit once, then stop! This makes determinates a great choice for canning when the crop is needed all at one time. Commercial canning factories use this kind. After its first (and only) crop the tomato plant is finished working. If you were expecting more fruits for the table, forget it.

Indeterminate varieties will keep you in sandwiches for months, and keep producing until frost kills them. They have sprawling vines that can reach more than ten or fifteen feet. They produce flowers at every second leaf, fruiting until the plant is finally killed by cold. They require some pruning to keep them a manageable size and to help the fruits mature to a larger size. The fact that indeterminates will keep producing until frost is, I think, the best bargain any gardener could find anywhere.

Stake the indeterminates or contain them in cages. The best type cage might be a 2- or 3-foot diameter cylinder made of sturdy galvanized wire. Stake each cylinder into the ground on two sides to prevent toppling over in wind storms. Wooden cages work very well but, in my gardening experience, I have found they don't last as long as the heavy wire ones do.

February

Checklist

✔ Check on the perennials that are in your garden beds. With winter's freezing, thawing and re-freezing, they have a tendency to heave out of the ground. Push them back in, making sure there are no exposed roots to dry out.

✔ Call the bakery ahead of time to order your *Faschnachts* (doughnuts) for Shrove Tuesday. Otherwise, you could be disappointed to find them sold out.

✔ Rotate houseplants a quarter turn at every watering. This prevents them from leaning and keeps them "well rounded."

✔ It's not too early to start this year's garden plans. Don't complain; you don't have to go out in the cold. Do it on paper from your recliner.

✔ Pull out your retired bean seed sprouter; visit the health food store for seeds, and give it a try. The fresh sprouts are just wonderful on sandwiches as a substitute for lettuce and in salads. And it lets you get busy growing green things again in the middle of winter.

✔ Are there Valentine flowers at your house? Remember to change the water every 2 or 3 days and display them out of direct sun and away from a heat source. (see *Be My Valentine*, February.)

✔ There may not be an ice-free watering place nearby for the wild birds that dine at your feeders. An immersion heater may be added to a birdbath or basin of water to keep it free of ice. Check at local hardware stores or where bird feeding supplies are sold.

✔ When doing your seed catalog shopping, try to include some little gems that you've never tried before, such as miniature vegetables and flower varieties and herbs that are new to you. Just make sure they are suitable for your growing conditions and zone.

✔ Prune fruit trees any time it's not too cold for you. February is a good time to cut back grapevines. Prune the darker-colored wood to encourage growth from the newer grape branches.

✔The full moon of February is called the Snow Moon. Don't put your snow shovels away yet; there is likely more to come.

✔During the winter when the house is closed up, the air can become dry, smoky or stagnant. Green foliage plants help improve air quality and even filter away such pollutants as benzene and tobacco smoke. The spider plant and bamboo are especially helpful in this regard, and orchids do their share better than many others.

✔Don't bother to fertilize house plants during winter months when daylight hours are at a minimum. Most of them enjoy a winter snooze (their dormant rest period) during that time.

✔Once paperwhites have bloomed they may as well be relegated to the compost pile, for forcing them for indoor bloom just once weakens them substantially.

✔The old saying goes, "When the crows fly" is the time to start tapping the back yard sugar maple tree. (see *Tap the Back Yard Maple Tree*, February.)

February Note: When the winter blahs get you down, invite a few friends to lunch. Serve wine and cheese, chicken salad with cold marinated asparagus, hot rolls with herb butter. Finish up with Cherry Cobbler and flavored teas. Then talk about your gardening plans for this year.

Plant hardiness Zones

In each of your seed catalogs (remember, they are valuable as reference books) you will always be able to find a United States Department of Agriculture Plant Hardiness Zone Map. It shows the United States divided into 11 zones that layer east-west, the lower number being the northern tier of states, and southward to Zone 11 in the tropical Florida Keys. Each zone represents the approximate average annual minimum temperature expected there. For example, most of southern and southeastern Pennsylvania lies within Zone 6 with the lowest average temperature of -10 to 0 degrees F.

Once you know your own growing zone, the rest is pretty much a snap. If I didn't know whether a plant I wanted would do well in my area, this Zone Map would give the information I need.

It is interesting to note that Zone 6 is a band that travels from sections of New England, through southeastern Pennsylvania, through sections of Virginia, West Virginia, all of Kentucky, into portions of Tennessee, Missouri, Kansas, Oklahoma, Texas into New Mexico. From there it squiggles northwestward through the Rockies to the state of Washington.

Zones overlap somewhat since elevation and exposure play a part in early or late frosts or in pockets that produce heat buildups. The Zone Map is only a guide for the gardener, but experience will reveal all the cold and warm spots that lie within your own garden.

According to the Pennsylvania State Cooperative Extension Service of Montgomery Country, PA, the Zone Map was developed in 1960 to assist farmers producing America's food, as well as home gardeners. Since then the map has been revised to reflect changes in stress factors, such as the prevalence of various kinds of pollution, security lighting and toxic wastes which have increased the potential for unsatisfactory performance of plants. The revised Zone Map also reflects new plant management systems that are widely practiced today using better planting, watering and fertilizing techniques.

Refer to the zone map whenever you lay out new plantings for your garden.

Flowers in the Snow

Adonis: You may be thinking it is too early for flowers to be blooming outside but look again. In the scheme of things, there are early bloomers and late bloomers.

What every garden in late winter needs, is what my neighbor, Geoffrey, has in his own garden.

He showed me a winter gem, the brazen little flower called Adonis, named for the mythical Greek figure who was slain by a wild boar. These lovely flowers were said to have bloomed where his blood spilled. Adonis (*Adonis vernalis*) is a perennial and in Zone 6 is usually the very first herald of spring, showing its brilliant yellow daisy-like blossoms to the late-winter sun. The short-stemmed flowers appear well before the ferny leaves do, opening fully to morning sunlight but closing their petals on cloudy days or in the afternoon shade. After the blossoms die back in several weeks' time, the developing leaves form a mound of green lace eight to ten inches high and a foot across.

The soil they prefer is light, composted and well-drained. Root division can be done in the spring right after blooming is completed. The leaves fade and die by mid-summer, making room for the next succession of flowers.

Snow Drops: (*Galanthus nivalis*) are the most modest of winter flowers. They are white, bell-shaped blossoms that nod on a four-inch stem. When blossoms have faded, large green berries appear at the top of the stem. When the berries have formed, it is your clue that it is time to separate the clumps. In just a few short years, the snow drop patch becomes crowded. If by autumn you have not divided the clump, you will find the crowded, tiny bulbs emerging from the soil to lie on top. This is your last chance to spread their joy in your landscape.

Snowdrops

Snowdrops are quite happy growing in full sun or full shade. They favor loose, composted soil, and will naturalize easily.

Aconite: Shy winter aconites (*Eranthis hyernalis*) are other early bloomers. These small, yellow-flowering plants that grow from a tuberous root, rises above last autumn's fallen leaves on collars of green. Related to the butter cup, they are not as showy as those of Adonis but warmly welcomed nevertheless, providing a steady flow of blossoms all February and March. Shop for these in late August and soak the bulbs overnight before planting. It is a good choice for shady gardens.

Hellebore: (*Helleborus orientalis*) Lenten Rose or Christmas Rose, is another early bloomer that benefits your garden as an easy-to-grow evergreen.

Hellebores have been cultivated for centuries in countries bordering the Mediterranean. Blossoms may be of cream color, green, rose or purple, or shades of rose-green, permeated with maroon dots. Blossoms are of five rounded petals with a central whorl of yellow stamens, much like the old favorite wild rose.

Leaves are deep green and palmate in shape and can be a foot across. Plants may be almost two feet tall, freely reseeding themselves into the surrounding soil to form colonies.

There are two down sides: All parts are poisonous to pets and humans alike, but deer are known to graze on it.

Lenten Rose prefers soil that is well-drained and composted. It needs a slightly alkaline soil, meaning that it can do quite well if planted near building foundations. Using a light layer of leaf mulch helps keep roots cool in the summer as well as protected in winter.

It thrives in locations where it can get winter sun but be shaded in summer, making it a perfect candidate to grow under or near deciduous trees.

I can see my own little colony of Lenten Roses from my windows, standing tall and green at a time of year when snow covers the ground.

One of the best attributes of Lenten Rose is that it offers a bounty of blossoms for little or no effort and is virtually pest-free. That makes it one of the winners in any late-winter, perennial garden.

What's in a Name?
A Lesson in Botanical Terms

Rose, bluebell, lily, daisy -- these names are lovely to contemplate but when talking to someone about any one of them, or finding exactly the one you want from catalog, common names are confusing and overlapping.

A gardener friend in Germany mentioned his profusion of Busy Lizzies. It took a lot of research to discover that Busy Lizzies are what I call impatiens. Other regional names for this same plant are Zanzibar, garden balsam, patience plant, sultana and patient Lucy.

How have botanists kept track of plant names? They developed a nomenclature system to accurately identify a plant, called the botanical name, usually of two parts. The first, the genus, always capitalized, identifies plants of one or more species with similar characteristics. These words come from Greek and Latin. When used in conjunction with the second name, the species, it provides the full, botanical description. The species name is a group of individual plants that share common attributes.

For instance, magnolia is a familiar genus. *Magnolia grandiflora*, as the second name implies, has large blossoms. In different regions it is known by the common name Southern or bull bay magnolia. The description M.g.'Little Gem' tells us that this large-flowering magnolia variety is one that has large flowers but has different growing habits. Variety is indicated by the single apostrophe before and after. The word variety is used to show variations that have occurred.

Hybridization? Another new word. A hybrid is a plant that has been created by cross-pollination of two species or varieties, usually of the same genus. Such improvements are then reproduced in ways other than by seeds so that offspring will be identical. Many of today's better flowering annuals are hybrids. Seeds from a hybrid will not produce a plant like its parent, but it can be reproduced by cuttings.

When you come across the term cultivar, what does that mean? It is a cultivated variety, the term used synonymously with variety.

After learning these new words you may go browsing through your garden catalogs with a little more confidence.

Dish Gardens for Everyone

Experiment by creating your own dish garden. It can be a good children's project, or one for you. The planting and care of a miniature indoor garden can satisfy any gardener's urge to keep something growing.

Any dish or bowl will do. Second-hand stores have large selections, or you may already have several potential containers at home. Since planters often have no drainage holes, a half-inch or one-inch layer of pebbles in the bottom is necessary.

Make a selection of 3 or 5 plants. But here's the most important part: The ones you choose should all have the same water and light requirements. Any greenhouse will have an assortment of small plants and they are usually labeled as to their particular needs.

Next, mix the sizes, textures and variations of leaf colors.

The plants you pick should remain small in size. A palm, for instance, may become three feet tall and the ivy four feet long. Look for ones that will remain small in stature, or use dwarf types. Consider dwarf ivies, small ferns, kalanchoes or cacti. African violets, begonias, wandering Jew, pothos, peperomia, are all good choices.

Place pebbles in the dish bottom. Fill with potting soil that is suitable to plant types. Plan the placement, then put them in. Soil can be mounded somewhat above planter rim. Tamp pieces of moss, small stones or pieces of rotted logs to create a pretty scene.

When watering, test for dryness by using a knife to probe beneath soil. Ideally, the soil beneath should be moist, never wet.

February Note: Flying Insect Traps are good for capturing indoor houseplant pests before they lay their eggs.

Bring Fresh Flowers to the Table

In January's Checklist I mentioned cuttings of pussy willow (*Glaucous willow*) for indoor arrangements. It is one of the very first harbingers of a long-awaited spring season. The children in my family have always delighted in cutting these branches from our ancient bush to "pet" the tiny willow buds that would grow fatter each day. Their teacher at school would welcome them for the classroom.

Thinking further along those lines, there are many other choices to consider when pussy willows are not available or the pussy willow idea wears out. Most spring flowering, woody plants are excellent candidates for cutting. These would include forsythia, all fruit trees (including quince if you are lucky enough to have one), spirea, wisteria, witch hazel, azalea, bridal wreath, red bud and lilac. And don't overlook the flower buds of rhododendron. Just a couple of them in a bowl with their rosettes of leaves make a striking display. They can be even more dramatic in a tall vase on a mantel or even on the floor.

When the weather turns mild for a few days, choose several medium-sized stems from any of the plants mentioned, looking for well-formed flower buds. Cut the stems on the diagonal, strip away the leaves and buds from the part of the stems that would be immersed in water. Hammer the ends or in some way crush them a little bit to allow full absorption of water. Now they can be put in a jar or vase in a cool place. Change the water every several days to prevent stagnation and odor. You will soon notice the buds will start swelling. It may take as little as 2, or as many as 6 weeks for the flower buds to open, depending on the plants chosen. When the flowers are ready to open, arrange them in tepid water and watch them do their thing.

If you like flowers as I do, one cutting will not be enough. I've taken a few cuttings every week for several weeks to keep a succession of flowers going throughout February.

Pest Portraits:

Cute Little Squirrels

We all know those little, grey animals with the bushy tails that hop around our yards and climb trees. (Did you know they are really rodents?) They create big, shaggy nests of leaves and sticks high in tree branches, looking rather like messy mop heads. Squirrels have two litters of young a year, one in the spring and the second one around September. They are entertaining to watch and when we go out to work in our yards, they will scold us for the interruption we have caused.

Squirrels are vegetarians, eating nuts, buds, fruits and sometimes breaking off new growth from shrubs and trees. They dig in the ground and can uncover newly planted bulbs (that they eat) and devour seeds from bird feeders. Many people feed them ears of dried corn, or cracked corn on the ground, but that only invites them to stay, making them fat and more productive.

They can wiggle their way into garages or homes to build cozy nests inside for the winter, where, un-noticed by you, they explore their inside domicile and eat insulation and house wiring. Then it's serious and time to call the exterminator.

Control of these clever pests is not always simple and takes some tactics on our part. To keep them away from newly-planted flower beds, lay pieces of chicken wire flat on the ground. They hate to walk on it. (This is suggested for rabbits and deer, as well.) In the summer the wire can be lifted for mowing, then replaced.

To keep them from nibbling on tender plants, a hot pepper spray can be used after every rain. To protect new growth on trees, wrap the trunks with a two-foot band of aluminum about five or six feet above the ground. This will keep them from climbing -- maybe.

They are animals that really should be employed by circuses, for they are also great leapers. If you discover that they are emptying birdfeeders before the birds get there, situate the feeders a good six feet from potential launching pads. If they would only empty the birdfeeders, that would be only one problem, but they often times chew through wood which results in serious damage or destruction of wooden feeders.

Squirrels are skillful acrobats and if you have defeated them in one way, they will soon figure out how to defeat you in another way. I have actually seen them strip rhododendron leaves off a main branch to provide themselves an unobstructed launching platform from which to leap onto the nearby hanging bird feeders.

Squirrel warfare can keep an otherwise dull winter very interesting.

Starting Your Own Tuberous Begonias

One of the most decorative blossoms of spring and summer comes from the tuberous begonia. Unlike the fibrous-rooted ones that we use as houseplants, these are tubers that are started in pots during late winter and produce plants that blossom from May until cold weather. The double-flowering, camellia-type blossoms come in shades of brilliant yellow, red, orange with newer varieties in romantic pastels. These begonias like moist, dappled shade. Even a sunny yard will have a shady corner somewhere -- under a tree or porch roof. They are great for hanging baskets or can be set right into a bed, window box or planter.

Garden centers have been receiving supplies of dormant begonia tubers this month. If a colorful display is what you have in mind and don't object to experimenting, now is the time to look for them and start some yourself.

Fill a pot with about three or four inches of growing medium. Place tubers onto the soil with the cup-shape up. The cupped surface is where the new shoots will come from while the roots will develop on the rounded surface of the bottom. Use one tuber per five- or six-inch pot, or if using a hanging planter that is larger, place them about three or four inches apart. Push them down until their tops are just below the soil surface and keep them moist but not wet.

When they start sprouting, cover with about one-half inch of soil and keep in a warm, sunny window. They will be doing most of their growing at this point and by the middle or end of May, will be in flower, ready to go outside.

When transferring to an outdoor bed, it may be better to leave them in their pots. Just sink the pots into the soil and cover up to the rims.

> *"Tuberous begonias are great for hanging baskets or can be set right into a bed, window box or planter."*

Throughout the spring and summer, the large flowers will drop as they mature. Keep them removed, for if they lie against foliage or stems, rotting can occur.

Try not to let these garden gems dry out. A wilted plant will be almost impossible to revive. At a friend's home I have seen the most profusely blossoming begonias ever, because he arranged a drip irrigation system that gave a gentle moisturizing every 24 hours. He also lightly fertilizes every two or three weeks throughout the flowering season. His plants always look like greenhouse specimens, and do him much credit as a gardener.

Take the Primrose Path

At this time of year nothing stops me in my tracks at a grocery store faster than a display of English primroses (*Primula vulgaris*) in bloom. The bright spring colors load me up visually and I linger, debating which colors are the best. At home, any color will look wonderful in any room. A couple of them of the same color nestled in a basket are even nicer.

While they remain indoors brightening our lives, they could use a little fertilizer every two weeks to prolong the bloom.

What happens after the blooming period is over? By that time spring has advanced and they can go right outside into the garden bed with the other perennials. I like to put mine in the borders. They are low-growing, take minimal care and can be depended upon to come back every year. That's a lot for a little investment.

It is good to keep in mind that they are shade-loving plants and do well in a damp or moist environment, such as on the north side of a home or under spreading trees. Place them along a path, in terra cotta tubs on a patio, in a flower bed among the forget-me-nots, bleeding hearts, or among ferns, hostas and other foliage plants. They are wonderful for rock gardens. Although they will not bloom for the rest of this year, their rosettes of crinkled leaves offer texture and will remain green throughout the summer. It is suggested that they will tolerate full sun if the soil remains moist, but I wouldn't chance it. Plant them in a part-shaded place.

When planting, prepare a hole and add several cups of compost. Loosen the plant from its container. The rootball may be compacted, so loosen that, too, and set the plant in the hole you've prepared. Fill in with the soil/compost mixture. Tamp lightly to squeeze out air pockets in the soil, then add water. Mulch helps maintain moisture and control weeds. Add it to a depth of about an inch or two. In dry weather, give your primroses a drink.

These English primroses will multiply all by themselves. When you see that they have formed large clusters after a year or two, divide. Just cut down vertically with a trowel and separate a few groups. Division can be done in the early spring or right after flowering. You will see that primroses have a way of multiplying your pleasures.

Of Weeds and Wildflowers
Skunk Cabbage

Although February seems too early to be talking about wildflowers, we can see that the first spring wildflower blossoms are already up and blooming while our world is still ice, snow and cold. Their fragrance will fill snowy woods with, not perfume, but rotting meat.

The blossoms are very strange-looking. Their purplish hoods, blooming in wetlands, will sometimes actually melt ice to do so. The hood we see is not a flower, but a conical spathe. The blossoms themselves are bunched inside on a short knob. This sounds kind of ugly. But these are characteristics of the arum family which includes calla lilies, philodendrons and the familiar Jack-in-the-pulpit.

Skunk cabbage (*Symplocarpus foetidus*) has a huge root system that is loaded with starch. By the end of January, the energy in this starch is used by the plant, raising the temperature inside the blossom to virtually 100 degrees. Sleeping insects are awakened and drawn to this heat and stench. They come to enjoy, and end up pollinating the plant. Smart? You bet. And it helps a lot that the color of the purplish spathe is just about the right color of spoiled meat.

By April the hoods wither away and the knob bends to the ground where it plants new seeds. By now the plant has sent up large, bright green leaves, and are often the first green we see in the spring forest. As the name promises, when these leaves are crushed or broken, they give off a smell that any one would recognize as the odor of skunk.

Skunk cabbage thrives in wet places, even roadside ditches, and is not very particular about other factors. It is probably the most common wetland plant. In late summer the large leaves die down, the roots are resupplied with energy for next winter's bloom and the cycle continues.

Be My Valentine

Valentine flowers are everyone's favorite. Because they can be expensive, it is important to know what to look for so the buyer can make the most of his purchase. The joy of receiving fresh flowers is equal to the joy of working with them to keep them fresh as long as possible.

After receiving a gift of cut flowers, it is important to replace the water every two or three days. In doing this, bacteria and odor will be virtually eliminated and the blossoms will stay beautiful for a longer period.

Where the arrangement is kept is important, too -- never on or near a radiator or fireplace where dry air will dehydrate them quickly.

Valentine roses are not the only floral gift. There are tulips, irises, sweet peas and violets.

When shopping for fresh-cut blossoms as a gift, it is the smart shopper who will check each bloom before buying. The petals should be free of bruises and the stems should have no broken or discolored leaves. Look to make sure that they have been kept in water while in the shop. If you find an arrangement that you like but it has a damaged flower or two, they should be replaced with fresh ones.

Roses, in particular, should be vibrant and healthy looking. If they are truly fresh, the buds will be partially open, slightly revealing the lovely spiraling of the petals. The heads should be standing stiff and tall, not nodding on weak necks. The rose blossoms to avoid would be those that are very tight, Hershey-kiss-type buds, for they will die just as they are without ever opening. Keeping these tips in mind is bound to insure satisfaction for the buyer and recipient, as well.

Where do florists' flowers come from? Some are grown in Florida and California and many are grown in hothouses locally. In recent years, South America has been a major supplier of roses of very good quality.

Tap the Backyard Maple Tree

When I discovered some sugar maples (*Acer saccharum*), in the back corner of my property, I was launched on a mission to tap and boil. Actually all maple trees produce sap but the sugar maple contains the highest percentage of sugar; hence, a little less boiling is involved.

The required spiles were hard to find. Those are the hard plastic spouts that are inserted into the tree trunk that allow sap to run from the tree, through the spile and into a jug. I found the spiles by calling a sugaring supply store in Michigan and I mail-ordered several.

We drilled a hole about two to three inches deep into the tree trunk about three feet above the ground, inserted the spile, attached a length of clear plastic tubing (from a medical supply store) and led the tubing to a gallon milk jug standing on the ground against the tree. Choose a tree with a trunk diameter of not less than 15 inches.

"Each tree generously gave me more than a gallon of sap a day."

Without the spiles, it is still possible to tap a tree, which I didn't know at the time. Drill a hole into the tree and insert the clear plastic tubing. Putty around it with grafting wax so there are no leaks. Lead the other end of the tubing into the gallon milk jug into which you have carved a hole near the top. Keep the hole small enough to accommodate the tubing. Keep a lid on the jug. Otherwise, snow, rain and dirt can wash into the jug.

I tapped 4 trees each winter for 4 winters. Each tree generously gave me more than a gallon of sap a day. Maximum sap production usually takes place in February or March. It is dependant on freezing temperatures at night, followed by warmer (35 to 40 degree) days. The old saying goes, "When the crows fly, it is time to start tapping the maple trees." But I observed that crows seem to fly all winter, so I judged by the calendar and by temperatures. In this section of Pennsylvania the season is short -- two or three weeks at most.

When tapping has stopped and the tubing is removed from the tree, the hole will heal rapidly. If this project is pursued next winter, you may not even be able to detect where the hole was. Do not look for it anyway. Drill a new hole and start your tapping experience all over again.

I enlisted the help of my granddaughters who loved to walk through the snowy woods to the maple trees to help lug the jugs back to the house. I discovered that the season is over when the sap stops flowing. That makes sense.

We really intended to boil the sap outside and rigged up an old refrigerator shelf on bricks which we planned to fire up with wood. For some reason we never got that far. However, I do strongly recommend that boiling and evaporating the sap should be done outside if at all possible. It can be a family or friend event with pop corn and hot cider. Jugs of fresh sap can be saved and refrigerated for a couple of days before processing, but no longer than that.

Many horror stories have been told about evaporating sap in the kitchen. I boiled it gently and had the steam go out the exhaust fan. I did have to clean the sticky sap from the stove hood once we finished. The sap remained on the stove for hours, evaporating, not actually boiling. If you do large quantities, then you may see wallpaper peeling off or threads of sugar hanging from the ceiling. We didn't boil that much.

It made precious little syrup (about one gallon of syrup for every 30 gallons of sap). But we shared it and had loads of fun.

We even drew charts, collected supplies and samples and presented a maple tapping program to the 3d grade at my granddaughter's school.

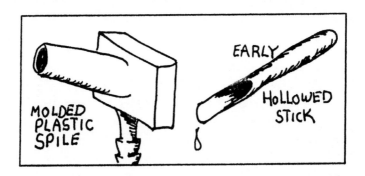

Different types of spiles that have been used for maple tapping.

herb of the Month
Lemon Balm

Once lemon balm (*Melissa officinalis*) gets into your gardens it happily spreads its seeds everywhere. I have pulled up dozens of volunteers where I didn't appreciate their company, leaving only those that I wanted. It's a member of the mint family and, like most mints, it will grow profusely and spread everywhere once established. Brush its leaves and you will enjoy an aroma of lemon with a minty undertone. It's blossoms draw bees, so brush carefully.

It can grow so profusely, it could be considered a nuisance, but it is an herb much underappreciated, so read up and get ready to welcome it this spring.

It is not particular about soil type, nor the attention it gets. It likes full sun but will do well in part shade. Besides self-sowing, it can be propagated by cuttings in water and by root division.

It has few enemy pests but may fall victim to powdery mildew. One way to treat this is to spray the plants with a hose , washing the spores away. Pay attention to the undersides of the leaves. Do this weekly until results are seen.

This plant has many uses in which you might be interested. Thomas Jefferson included lemon balm in his gardens at Monticello. It is used as an ingredient in Old Williamsburg recipes as well as herbal teas breads. Its leaves can be chopped or used whole in fresh fruit dishes, meat salads, salad dressings, as sprigs in iced drinks or baked with fish. Crush fresh leaves and rub on the skin to repel flies and mosquitoes. Used as tea, lemon balm has a calming, relaxing effect. Use like regular tea leaves, steeping about five or six minutes. If a stronger brew is desired, do not increase steeping time but add more leaves. Oversteeping causes bitterness. Experiment with quantities until you've got it just the way you like it.

Harvest leaves in the morning after the dew has dried. Once the plant blooms, cease harvesting. Lemon balm is used fresh in many recipes, but it can be dried by picking leaves off of the stems and drying them in single layers on paper towels on a cookie sheet to enjoy in wintertime, too.

African Violets

If carefree, easy-going house plants are for you, do not overlook African violets (*Saintpaulia ionantha*). They bloom from spring through autumn and can tolerate heated, dry homes. Now how can anyone pass up an agreeable plant like that?

The early ones years ago were deep blue-purple with bright yellow anthers. I grew up with several of these blue-purple beauties in each room of the house which my mother tended carefully.

The variety of colors and shapes are so numerous now, it is hard to decide which is nicest, for growers have developed pinks, lavenders, whites. There are frilled, speckled, striped and double blossoms. The leaves are as variable, being reddish-hued or ivory on the undersides, small or large, deeply quilted, glossy or dull or ruffled. If you are undecided which one is best, try several. I always like two or three such plants grouped together in a basket, creating a greater visual impact.

Use ordinary flowering house plant fertilizer at half-strength. No need to buy special products for them.

It is not necessary that they be watered only from the bottom as was believed long ago. They may receive water from the top just so long as care is taken that their leaves or crown do not become wet. Just lift a leaf or two and add water to moisten the soil. Watering once or twice a week is usually all that is necessary.

African violets are actually forest plants. They require bright light but without full sun. In the summer a north light is best. Other times of year, sunny spots are fine if the sun is filtered by something like a curtain.

Breaking off a mature leaf at the base of the plant and suspending it in water through an aluminum foil support or one devised of plastic wrap is a way to produce more plants, keeping the leaf dry above the foil, and the stem below the foil in water. After little roots appear it is time to pot them in 2-inch pots in African violet soil, leaf humus or compost. When potbound, they can be transferred into 3- to 4-inch containers where they will now begin to bloom.

African violets will also form their own new plantlets right in the pot and become crowded. In that case, it is easy to remove them with a sharp knife and replant the new ones in their own pots.

Checklist

✔ Sunshine! Month of the vernal equinox. About mid-March is spring cleaning time in the yard and garden. Rake away winter debris and get rid of old leaves, dead foliage and old stalks.

✔ After we have all this debris collected, what is to be done with it? Compost it, of course, if you feel quite sure it is free of disease and pests (see *Really Dirt Cheap*, March).

✔ In pulling out old leaves from between and behind shrubs, an ordinary garden rake doesn't seem to fit. Invest in a shrub rake -- much smaller -- which fits easily into tight areas.

✔ Order your supply of mulch to apply to the cleaned garden beds. (see *Removing the Mystery of Mulch*, April.)

✔ Your beds will look very professional if time is taken to do some edging. Grass roots often encroach into beds. An edger is a useful tool that puts on a finishing touch. Mine is just a semi-circular slicing blade at the end of a long handle that is easy to use.

✔ Look over the iris bed. Borers love careless housekeeping. Clean away all dead foliage, cutting with scissors or clippers.

✔ In the early spring and again in the fall are good times for fertilizing acid-loving plants -- azaleas, hollies, rhododendrons, blueberries, evergreens, pachysandra, lily of the valley, dogwoods, ferns.

✔ Extreme winter temperatures take a toll of branch tips. Browned tips on small shrubs indicate winterkill. Cut them back to about a half-inch of the next set of twigs. If most branches have been affected, resign yourself to buying replacements.

✔ Shrubs can suffer breakage from ice or snow buildup. Prune off jagged, broken ends making a smooth, clean cut. Otherwise, rain water will collect that could attract insects and decay.

✔ Have you been walking on your soggy lawn? It is best not to; use the walks instead. Soil that is soggy-wet compacts easily and is harder for grass roots to send out new shoots. Compaction may even kill some grasses.

✔Onions can be put into the vegetable garden any time now, providing the soil does not flunk that "squeeze" test! (see *To Dig or Not to Dig?*, April.)

✔When picking out onion sets from the store choose ones that are among the smaller-sized. They will grow the best bulbs. Larger ones (of about nickel size or larger) tend to develop thick necks and go to seed quickly. However, if they are included in a pre-packaged bag, use them anyway. They can be pulled early as scallions.

✔ Tradition has it that peas can be planted on St. Patrick's Day, but as long as you do it any time *before* mid-April, you'll still get a good crop.

✔House plants have had a long winter snooze and are responding to lengthening daylight, so get the fertilizer going this month. Fish emulsion mixed according to bottle directions is a big boost.

✔In raking up the garden beds near the house or along walls, you may uncover carpenter ants that have, unknown to you, created a colony in the vicinity. If so, it is time to call the exterminator for advice.

✔Pansies can be set out, even in cold soil. They prefer low temperatures and will bloom steadily if spent blossoms are removed.

✔Check birdhouses to give them a cleaning. Tenants should be arriving any time.

✔Lawn furniture may need repair or repainting. Schedule such jobs before it is time to put them to regular use.

✔If the compost pile has been neglected over the winter, get it going with a dose of manure, some left-over mulch from garden beds, leaves or straw, and get it turned. Then it's ready to go.

> *"If the grass looks greener on the other side of the fence -- fertilize."*
> Voice of Health Magazine

Seed Starting Made Easy

The reason for starting your own seeds is that you get to choose varieties you've never had before, or ones that you know you liked and want to use again.

Perhaps by now your seed catalog shopping has been done. Also, many stores have their seed packets now at greatly reduced prices -- too good to pass by. Once the seed packets are in your hands, it's easy to say, "Hey, let's plant!" Check the seed packets for length of germination time, the last frost-free date in your area that seedlings can be set out and for days to maturity. Last frost date for southeastern Pennsylvania and Zone 6 is May 15. Count the days backward to find out approximately when to start your seeds. If outdoor planting time is mid-May, many seeds can be started indoors by the end of March. No sense getting the planting urge too early because if your seedlings are grown and ready to go outside when it's still frosty, that won't do.

Now that you've got an idea of a starting date, the process of starting seeds indoors is easy -- seeds are programmed to know what they're supposed to do -- sprout. But once they sprout, things can become tricky if you don't know what to

> "Seeds are programmed to know what they're supposed to do -- sprout."

look for. Before you know it, they could dry out or just fall over from damp off. They can also grow into very tall, skinny things that will be weak. Overcoming these small obstacles is simple. Here's how.

Look over the seed-starting systems in garden centers. There are several methods that can be used to start seeds, and they all work. One that I have used very successfully is the black plastic double trays. Two or more seeds get put into each little cubicle on top of pre-moistened seed-starting medium. The seeds then get covered with a light layer of medium and misted with a spray bottle. These inexpensive bottles are available at many dollar or garden stores. I cover my black plastic trays with kitchen plastic wrap to hold in moisture until I see about half of the seedlings starting to emerge.

The biggest factor now becomes light. Many seeds do not need light to sprout, but once they break through their protective coating, they need all the light they can get. That means 12 to 15 hours a day. Natural daylight is not long enough once they have started sprouting. A four-foot shop light rigged up over my planting table in the cellar provides enough light to make about 5 to 6 dozen plants sturdy and green. It's not even necessary to install expensive grow lights. The regular fluorescent tubes will do fine, providing their height is adjustable to be suspended over the planting trays about 3 to 5 inches above the plants. We rigged ours up on two chains with S-type curtain hooks that allow the light to be easily raised as the plants grow taller.

Seedlings should be looked in on only once a day, but I get so inspired by this growing phenomenon that they see my face several times a day. They should be watched for signs of drying out. A foolproof method of keeping them moist is with the mister bottle. The planting medium should be kept moist, but not soggy. Your practiced eye will tell you when either of those conditions is present. Make sure that only one plant is growing in each cubicle, snipping off the smaller or less happy ones.

Watch for the first "true" leaves. Those come after the initial two have sprouted. About two weeks later, start applying half-strength fertilizer. Use this every week for about three weeks. After that, full-strength solution can be applied every two weeks. Keep notes when these applications are made, or decide on a schedule such as the first and 15th of each month, etc.

When three or four sets of leaves have developed, transplant from their little cubicles to a larger pot. I use left-over foam coffee cups with a pencil hole punched in the bottoms. Peat pots from the store are fine also. Almost anything will do.

Before moving the seedlings, make sure the soil is moist. Fill the new containers part way up with new potting soil. Loosen each plant with a label stick or craft stick, carefully lifting the whole soil mass into the new pot, disturbing roots as little as possible. Tamp additional new soil around and fertilize once more, keeping them uniformly moist. The trays that are now empty can be rinsed off and stored until next year.

Your seedlings will be ready to harden off during the first half of May, depending on the weather. This may be another tricky time for them. Look in May's chapter for *Hardening Off.*

Did Someone Mention Rhubarb?

L et's talk briefly about one of the earliest vegetable crops to appear in gardens. Early gardeners eagerly looked forward to rhubarb's appearance to help break the tedium of winter-long dried and preserved foods. It was one of the first fresh foods of the year on family tables.

In the early spring the rosy knobs and tips of rhubarb are ready to emerge. Pull away the mulch that you have placed around each plant and scratch a 10-10-10 fertilizer into the soil. Replace the mulch and add more if necessary. This covering will keep roots moist and cool later on in summer heat. If starting new plants, they should be put into well-composted soil, about one inch below the surface and spaced about 2 ½ feet apart. Harvesting of new plants shouldn't take place until the third year. As summer heat comes on, flower stalks will form. Keep these cut off and let all the plant's energy go to the roots and development of good stalks.

Thick stalks about 12 to 18 inches long are ideal for harvest. Always pull the stalks away from the outer edges of each plant, never from the center. The center of the plant is where all the new growth takes place. To disturb that center core may spell doom for the entire plant.

If your older plants have been producing only slim stalks, it may be time to divide. Do so right now or wait until autumn. Dig up the whole plant, cut it into two or three sections and replant. The new divisions should not be planted in any place where they will be disturbed by work with annuals.

Bear in mind that the leaves of rhubarb are high in oxalic acid and considered toxic to consume. They should be totally stripped off the stalks, but are perfectly safe to be added to the compost pile.

There are some good green varieties to grow which are every bit as good as red ones, but the reds (*Ruby, Valentine, MacDonald*) make prettier desserts. You would find no difference in taste or flavor between the two colors.

Our family enjoys stewed rhubarb on breakfast toast. I add several slices of lemon during cooking, then remove it when cooking is completed. The flavor is delicious.

Rhubarb Upside Down Cake

My friend Elizabeth gave me a recipe for a rhubarb upside down cake. This is from her mother in Wisconsin where they enjoy it every spring. It has become everybody's favorite in our family.

In a round, 9-inch pan or large iron skillet, place:
3 cups chopped rhubarb, sprinkled with 3/4 cup sugar, sprinkled over top of that with 100 miniature marshmallows.

Cake:
½ cup margarine (can be low-fat)
3/4 to 1 cup sugar
2 eggs beaten
1 3/4 cup flour
1/4 tsp. salt
3 tsp. baking powder
½ cup milk

Combine as you would for any cake (creaming the margarine and sugar; adding the eggs, then dry ingredients alternately with milk) and pour or spoon over filling in pan. Bake at 350 degrees for 45 to 60 minutes. Cool in pan about five minutes before inverting onto platter.

Really Dirt Cheap
(Composting)

K itchen greens, coffee grounds, fruit peels, corn cobs and almost everything that takes up space in your trash can be reduced to compost, a superior ingredient of garden soil. And it reduces the volume of trash leaving your house for the landfill. When composted, all these organic wastes turn magically into a black gold type of earth. *Organic* is the key word here. Not admitted to the compost club are the non-organics or things of animal origin -- all dairy products and meat by-products such as bones, skin and fat.

Start your compost pile in an area out of the way, yet near enough to the kitchen door so you can run out and add your organics throughout the year.

Start the pile with a layer of "browns." These would be dry ingredients such as leaves or shredded newspapers. Next comes a layer of small sticks and twigs to add aeration, then a layer of "greens" such as the kitchen peelings and grass clippings. Cover that with a thin layer of soil, old mulch or manure, and your compost pile is in business.

Black vinyl bins, at a nominal cost, are available at stores and through your County Extension Service. A more elaborate system of wooden bins with sliding doors looks neater perhaps, and it works. A "free-form" pile can be placed in an unobtrusive spot right on the ground, and it works, too.

Do not locate it directly under trees. Tree roots have a way of insinuating themselves into the pile, leaving you with a matted mess.

Keep the top of the pile slightly concave in order to catch rain water because moisture is another key ingredient. Add ingredients at any time. With something like a pitchfork or mulch fork, turn the pile every week or so. Takes just a minute or two, and it is not usually heavy work.

Take note here that if the pile develops insects such as fruit flies, it's probably because you are guilty of "dumping and running." Fruit will attract flies which will establish a colony rapidly and will seem to never go away. Keep the turning fork handy so when something sweet like fruit is added, it can be turned under right away.

Sometimes during the winter, we stop adding to the pile. To get it active again in the spring, add a dose of manure, some mulch material from beds, leaves or straw, then give it a good turning. Note whether it seems dry. If so, use the hose to wet it through and help it on its way.

You will be surprised by this garden chemistry in action. Completed compost can be raked out of the bottom and used for plantings and even in pots for house plants. They love it.

Composting Do's and Don'ts

Do Add:

Grass clippings

Vegetable and fruit peels and trimmings

Shredded newspaper

Old straw

Horse, cow, chicken or rabbit manure

Twigs and sticks from yard cleanup

Wood ashes in small amounts

Sawdust (but NOT from Pressure-treated wood)

Garden prunings

Corn stalks, husks and cobs

Tea bags and leaves (no strings)

Wood chips (but NOT from walnut trees)

Old flower pot soil

Pine needles

Kitty litter (unused!!)

Coffee grounds and paper filters

Spent flowers, stalks, leaves

Egg shells, rinsed

Peanut shells

Don't Add:

Dog and cat manure

Weeds with seeds

Meat or fish parts

Dairy products

Dishwater

Cigarette ashes or butts

Walnut leaves or husks

Diseased plants

Invasive weeds

Kitchen oils or grease

Magazine paper

Barbecue charcoal ashes

Coal ashes

Chalk it up to Chard

Swiss chard (*Beta vulgaris*) is a versatile vegetable that is grown for its leaves and stems. It is a member of the goosefoot family, which includes beets and spinach. Its stems are thick and leaves large, both of which yield exceptional salads or stir fries. Some recipes call for chard stems only, used as raw vegetable dippers or sliced like celery and creamed as a hot dish. Leaves can be cooked and served just as spinach would be. If chard wasn't in your plans this year, plan again.

Before a new variety called Bright Lights came along, the only choices of this plant were the variety with white stems or Ruby chard which has bright red stems. Both are still available, but since the advent of Bright Lights, why not "go for the gold"? Its stems glow in electric colors of yellow, gold, violet, orange, pink and crimson.

This particular vegetable does not have to be relegated to the vegetable bed. It is classed as an ornamental to be shown off among flowers or as a centerpiece in a planter.

Besides being amazingly colorful, it is good-tasting. But wait, there's more. It is heat tolerant and that is why you will be able to harvest your chard throughout the summer heat when other leafy vegetables have started to fail.

It is a hungry grower, needing lots of feeding. Dig in plenty of aged manure before planting. Once the plants are six inches high, feed with 5-10-5 fertilizer every four weeks. Space the plants about ten inches apart. Eliminate weeding by mulching. Harvest leaves from the outer edges, leaving the centers to produce more stalks. Just break off the stems at the base. Don't use a knife, as it may injure inner stems.

Striped cucumber beetles may appear in hot weather. Hand pick and destroy eggs clinging to leaf undersides. Leaf miners also attack chard. At the first sign, remove the affected leaves to prevent adult flies from multiplying. If aphids appear, rinse away with a spray from the hose.

You will enjoy growing this bright vegetable.

herb of the Month
Horseradish

Many gardeners do not consider horseradish an herb, but a condiment. In reference books, it is called a medicinal herb. It is a native of southeastern Europe, is a member of the cabbage and mustard family with tough, white roots. It requires full sun. The leaves usually grow two to three feet long and the plant can spread up to 18 inches wide. Its flowers are small, creamy white clusters. This herb can sometimes be found growing in the wild.

If you have not yet ventured forth with a horseradish crop, do so.

Chose a corner of the garden where it will not be not interplanted with other crops. In soft garden loam it will burgeon and take over. In poor soil it will simply do well and not disappoint you. Most growth occurs in late summer. It is ready to harvest in October or November. Dig its roots out carefully with a fork.

Reserve some main root sections several inches long and store in sand in a dark closet or cellar. These can be planted next spring for the next crop. I opt to leave some root cuttings right in the ground when I harvest and they have grown well again the following year.

The roots will often invade other plants if not removed by harvesting every year. Be forewarned that if you are trying to get rid of it in a garden, it comes back every spring like a party crasher. Keep pulling it out until every last scrap of viable root has been extracted.

Happily for us, its presence in the garden discourages several fungal diseases and is known to repel blister beetles.

Meanwhile, after harvesting roots, take them to the kitchen for washing, peeling and grinding in the blender with a little white vinegar or white wine vinegar.

After grinding, avoid peering into the container or sniffing it. The bite will reach your eyes and nose and the effect can be staggering! Close it up in jars and store in the refrigerator.

Regarding its medicinal properties, it's been used for centuries as a diuretic and as a compress for neuralgia relief. Hoarseness of the throat has been relieved by a syrup made of honey and grated horseradish. And I can personally confirm that it clears a stuffy nose instantly!

Another Kind of Radish

Here's another kind of radish for you and one that I always plant early because it's a good excuse to get outside after a winter indoors. No one in my family likes radishes, so I grow these just for myself -- my special treat. I like them especially when sliced up in a thick sandwich (preferably on rye bread) with mayonnaise and a liberal application of salt (optional).

Radishes are a good crop for little gardeners (children in your family) because the seeds are big enough not to get lost. They germinate rapidly in a wide range of moisture conditions so are almost fool proof to grow. In three or four weeks the little red globes are ready to harvest. What could be more satisfying for a young gardener?

Some seed packets offer a mix of radishes which are fun to use for beginners. It helps the gardener become acquainted with the many different varieties and generates a lot of interest to see what kind is coming up out of the ground next.

After sprouting, they should be thinned to stand an inch or two apart to allow space for globe formation. Two weeks after emergence, they start to fill out their roots. For a continuous spring harvest, plant more every ten days or so.

When mature, pull radishes promptly. They are at peak for only a few days. Spring radishes don't like sitting around the kitchen, so bag them and keep in the crisper drawer. There, they will last until the next ones mature. By the time all are harvested, the empty space in the garden will welcome the summer vegetables.

It is interesting to note that the radishes harvested early will be mild in flavor. By the time your last ones are harvested, they are likely to be as hot as firecrackers. Why? Watering and abundant spring rains keep them mild; stress from drier soil and higher temperatures, as spring turns to summer, heats them up!

Insect Insights
Whitefly, Mealybugs and Red Spider Mites

Houseplants during the indoor season sometimes develop insect infestations. In bringing your house plants indoors in the early autumn, you may have also brought in some passengers in the form of insect pests. You may have washed the plant leaves off with a fine spray from the hose, and you may also have submerged the whole pot into water for a long soak before bringing in. But there could still be some insects that escaped your treatment.

These may be whitefly or mealybugs. They live outside and come in on otherwise clean plants. Once they gain a foothold they will flourish. The dry, heated atmosphere of a home in winter is just what they like. If they escape your notice early, they may become entrenched. Once one plant is infected, the insects often spread to neighboring plants.

Whitefly is just what the name implies. White flies. Tiny, about 1 mm long, they are difficult to see until branches or foliage are disturbed. Then they fly up suddenly before settling down again. Eggs, tiny grey and yellow cones, are laid on the undersides of leaves. They hatch into larvae which appear as tiny scales. They also cling to undersides of leaves, and while they feed, they are sucking the juices from your plant, causing yellowed leaves that drop. They also secrete a sticky honeydew which can host a sooty mold. That will be another clue that they are present.

> *"The dry, heated atmosphere of a home in winter is just what they like."*

A household insect spray can be used to control the flies, but the eggs are not susceptible and will hatch into another generation. This means more spraying. Another option is to use an insecticidal soap once a week. Applications for several weeks should show good results. Yet another choice is to use gloves to rub the eggs and larvae off as many leaves as possible, and/or use yellow sticky traps to capture the winged adults until the problem is solved.

Mealybugs are grey or white fluffy ovals about 2.5 mm long. If watched, they can be seen moving, but mostly, they stay in one place to eat. Like whitefly larvae, they suck plant juices. The fluffy pieces are the females; the males are tiny winged insects that are rarely seen. Like the whitefly, mealybugs leave a trail of honeydew. Their eggs, and laid in clusters of up to 600 at a time, and hatch in about 10 days. The larvae crawl away looking for a good place to picnic, usually in joints or along stems of the plant.

Control is to knock them off with a spray of water in a sink or tub. In addition, a cotton swab soaked in alcohol can remove the rest. Just apply alcohol wherever you see them hiding in crevices and joints, and at the soil line. It won't hurt the plants. Several of these search-and-destroy missions with the alcohol swab will probably be necessary.

> "Diligent monitoring pays off, both with indoor and outdoor plants."

Plants that are bought at any nursery or greenhouse should come home pest-free, but just in case you end up with one that harbors trouble, you, the customer, should request an exchange for a healthy specimen, or a refund.

Diligent monitoring pays off, both with indoor and outdoor garden plants to catch problems while they are still small. This saves a lot of effort on your part, and easily saves a plant from failing, perhaps beyond redemption.

Red Spider Mites are another common houseplant pest. Just like the two previously-mentioned insects, they feed on the plant juices. They are tiny, red spiders that weave a fine web around the place where they are feeding. Their feeding weakens the plant and causes mottling of leaves and leaf drop.

The remedy to rid your plants of this pest is to spray with water, usually easiest done in a sink or tub, or use an insecticidal soap spray. A few weekly applications should remove the red spider mite problem.

Clinging Vines

Flowering vines are often not the prize of the garden but they play an important role in many ways. They can be called the Special Effects Department.

Vines can be used to act as a shield or screen against sun or for privacy. They act as camouflage to hide trash cans, propane tank or compost pile. On a trellis they add greenery and color to tool sheds or can enhance old fences. On an arbor they can shelter a picnic table or soften a masonry wall. If you think about it, you probably have at least a few places where a flowering vine would fill the bill.

Not all vines climb in the same manner. For instance, some twine around a support like sweet peas which can wrap a tendril around a pole. Wisteria twists its entire stem or branch around for support. English ivy and wintercreeper use little adhesive rootlets, while Boston ivy and Virginia creeper have adhesive pads at the ends of their tendrils. These last four mentioned, not flowering, are excellent for covering masonry walls. Climbing roses are different for they have no real way of holding on. They just sprawl and need help to push canes through a trellis and tie in place.

Many people believe that vines should never climb brick or stone walls because they destroy the mortar. It has not been proven to be so. If a wall has lost its integrity, the vines do seek crevices to enter. As they grow, the crevice is enlarged. Otherwise, they do no damage. Do keep them out of rain gutters and off roof edges, for some vines creep under shingles and loosen gutter fastenings.

The flowering vine I grew up with is the old-fashioned clematis which bears clusters of small white flowers in the autumn. It is still available in garden stores but is not as popular as the newer hybrids that feature large flowers in bright colors. Many are seen beautifying a mailbox, lamp post or porch trellis.

The annual sweet pea (*Lathyrus odoratus*) is a favorite. It too is fragrant and blooms in early summer in shades that range through blue-pinks and whites, changing shades as the blossoms age.

The annual black-eyed Susan vine (*Thunbergia alata*) will climb a trellis or ramble contentedly along the ground. Blossoms have dark eyes and petals of bright gold, orange and creamy white.

Do not dismiss the common morning glory (*Ipomoea purpurea*), which some call an alien invasive, without considering its beauty. It comes in pretty shades of purple, pink, white or deep red. Some blooms are streaked with other colors. It grows well on trellises, arbors or gazebos and will bloom all summer.

Scarlet runner bean (*Phaseolus coccineus*) produces not only scarlet flowers all summer, but edible green beans as well. In this country we grow it as a flower. Visiting friends from England were horrified that we largely disregard the edible beans. We were scolded for not being more thrifty.

Purple bell vine *(Rhodochiton atrosanguineum)* will grow six feet or more and presents interesting flowers throughout the summer. The nodding, bell-shaped flowers contain a black-purple flower within a pink-maroon calex. After the purple-black flowers fade, the pinkish bells continue to dangle on the plant.

Trumpet vine should not be overlooked (*Campsis radicans*). It is a tough, vigorous plant, producing numerous long, orange or red trumpet flowers which attract hummingbirds all summer. It is excellent for a screen for it conceals quickly and can actually become rampant. Pruning keeps it under control.

Add interest to any corner of your yard with these lovely summer vines.

Of Weeds and Wildflowers
Dandelion

The dandelion (*Taraxacum officinale*) is one of the most perfect plants that ever evolved. It is known as a common lawn annoyance, but in other circles, has been highly respected for its contribution to the human need. Its roots, leaves and flowers have culinary, cosmetic and medicinal uses, plus it is used as a dye plant.

It grows in any temperate zone, in any kind of soil and in full sun or even partial shade. It is a perennial that has a very long tap root. When pulling dandelions from our yards, if even a scrap of that tap root is left in the ground, that same plant will continue growing and blooming again. The leaves are as nutritious as any green leafy vegetable and used as such in many European countries. If the leaves are taken while still very young their taste is mild but when left to age, they turn somewhat zesty in flavor. For some, this zestiness is sometimes preferred in salads when mixed with other greens. The leaves have also been used in recipes of some herbal beers.

Dandelion can be cooked as a vegetable, using the very young rosettes that grow just at the soil surface in early spring. The roots can be dried or used fresh, chopped, in a tea sweetened with honey as a nutritious tonic. My great grandmother in the coal-rich mountains of Pennsylvania was the local herbalist. She gathered and grew many herbs for healing. Always included in her herbal pharmacy was dried dandelion root.

Centuries ago European women infused the flowers in water to use as a facial rinse to diminish freckles. This infusion was also used in herbal baths.

Very interestingly, the blossoms create a yellow dye for woolens, but use of the whole plant creates a magenta color.

Its blossoms, when mature, create what some like to call a "blow ball". The seeds from this pretty blow ball sail into the air and can stay aloft for days until brought down by rain. Wherever they land is where they will sprout.

Alas, today we have very little respect for this useful plant except to experiment occasionally with the making of dandelion wine.

Dandelion Wine

Over a period of many years, fellow-gardener and historian, Ron Treichler, has collected dandelion wine recipes and has tried every one of them. The recipe that follows has been deemed by Mr. Treichler as just about the best he has come across. It happens to be very close to one that was included in his grandmother's hand-written "receipt" book.

This manuscript recipe was published in the Goschenhoppen Historians, Inc. (Green Lane, PA) Folk Festival Recipe Book in 1980, exactly as the writer put it down on paper.

Dandelion Wine

Take 6 qts dandelion blossoms
Take 4 qts water
Soak 3 days and 3 nights
Strain
Add 4 lbs white sugar
　　　3 sliced oranges
　　　3 sliced lemons
　　　2 tbs or 2 cakes dry yeast
Let stand 4 days and 4 nights.
Strain
Bottle, do not tighten caps until all fermentation stops. It may take 2 - 3 weeks depending on temperature and quantity. It gets good around Christmas.

What's this
Planting by the Moon Phases?

Many people believe that good gardening is influenced by the phases of the moon. A rule of thumb is to plant all root crops when the horns of the moon are pointing downward in the third or fourth quarter. That is called the "dark of the moon" and it occurs from the day after a full moon until the day before it is new again.

The opposite is true for all plants that produce their yield above ground. When the horns are pointing upward, it is their time. This period is called "light of the moon" or "increase of the moon," and occurs from the day the moon is new until the day it is full. This explains why it is helpful to have an almanac or clock or calendar that shows moon phases. Of course, an optional method is to look at the night sky if there is no cloud cover, and not confuse the waxing or waning phases. That takes a lot of attention on the gardener's part.

Whether planting seeds indoors for sprouting or outside directly into the ground, the "horns of the moon" theory still prevails.

My husband's grandfather planted by the moon phases. He was a renowned gardener in his community and practiced many good gardening techniques throughout the early 20th century. Whether the moon was his primary factor for success is unknown; no one ever argued about his gardening accomplishments.

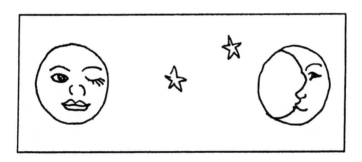

April

Checklist

✔Overcrowded irises fare better if thinned. Remove clumps of rhizomes, sorting through for rotting. *Discard those that seem unhealthy. Replant with bottom of the rhizome directly in contact with the soil and the upper part uncovered.

✔Stands of phlox benefit from division, as well. Every 3 years (or so) divide each plant into clumps and dispose of the older, center sections. Divide hostas and primroses, as well, if clusters have become too large.

✔Assemble garden tools that were relegated to the far corners of garage or tool shed when snow shovels came out. If they were stored muddy, shame on you! Work them clean and slightly oil the metal parts.

✔Paint the ends of garden tool handles bright red, or some color that stands out. They can be found quickly if laid down and you will always know which tool is yours if it has been loaned out.

✔Often, stubborn weeds become embedded in roots of a perennial. Pull the weeds out as often as possible but if any small piece remains in the soil, it will grow again. Then the only choice may be to lift out the whole plant, separate the roots, remove the weed, and replant.

✔At garden centers thousands of bedding plants will be there from which to choose. Avoid buying those that are already in full bloom, for they take a little longer to become established in your growing environment than younger ones still in bud.

✔Old clay pots can harbor harmful, soil-borne organisms. Scrub any dirt off in a tub of soap-and-water solution, then soak 15 minutes in a second solution of one part bleach to nine parts water. Rinse. Plastic pots should be treated, as well.

✔Early this month, take advantage of April showers. Sprinkle grass seed in the lawn's bare spots, raking the soil first to give new seeds a foothold. Keep evenly moist until fully sprouted. If they dry out for just a day or two, mortality rate can be high.

✔Take heart, gardeners. You should never be discouraged if something you want to grow doesn't do well for you. It may take a little experimenting to find the right location and combination of conditions such as light, moisture and soil.

✔ Look at your journal from last year to refresh your memory and let it be a guide to your planting dates this year. (see *Garden Journal,* April.)

✔Try something different. Stagger some large pots (not less than four inches deep) on sunny steps or a walkway and sow little crops of lettuce or radishes. They will be handy when needed.

✔If buying seedling trees by mail order or from a local tree seedling program, plant them in a "nursery" area until their stature becomes such that they can stand on their own in a lawn without being cut down by mistake.

✔What does "good" soil look like? It is light, soft, crumbly and airy. This condition is always one to be worked toward. Regular applications of compost and other organic materials go far in creating this ideal.

*Discard: This means any plant material that is deemed by you to contain damaging insects or disease should be bagged and treated as trash. No self-respecting compost pile would welcome it.

Get in Shape

For those of us who are beginning to feel our years, or those of us who have become couch potatoes during the winter, don't let gardening be a pain this season. Once mild, sunny weather comes it is easy to want to spend hours and hours outside. Be careful to avoid all-day marathons. Start gradually. Mild stretching and toning exercises are beneficial before throwing your weight into the pitchfork or shovel.

For moving large or multiple items, expect to use a cart or wheelbarrow, letting wheels do the work. Aching knees -- or worse yet, damage to knees -- can be avoided by using strap-on kneeling pads. Otherwise, folded towels, carpet scraps or latex foam can be used. Raised garden beds bring the garden up a little closer so less stooping may be required.

"Don't let gardening become a pain this season."

Everyone should learn the lifting rule in using the knees and not the back to lift objects from ground level. Keeping the back straight, flex at the knees to grab hold of the load and use the knees to carry the weight as you straighten up.

Get into the habit of a daily walk to limber up for only 15 or 20 minutes at a time. Daily walking is a whole-body conditioner. Every little bit helps and gives a feeling of well-being while preparing for a glorious season ahead of gardening.

Spring Azaleas

You may have received a potted azalea (*Rhododendron*) as a gift or bought a few for yourself. Azaleas are field grown, hardy and virtually pest-free. Technically, they can be planted outside this month but there is risk of frost damage to blossoms. Keep them inside for now to enjoy to them fully. After mid-May (see *Last Frost Date*, April), they can go outside in their permanent spot and will become a lasting part of your landscape.

Easter Lilies

Another welcome spring plant is the white Easter lily (*Lilium longiflorum*). Do not discard it after it is finished blooming indoors, for there are years of life left in it.

Cut the blossoms off as they fade; otherwise, seed heads will form, weakening the bulb. After the top dies down, the bulb can be removed from the pot and planted outside. Place it in a hole deep enough for the tip of the bulb to be 3 or 4 inches below soil surface. Choose the right spot with some forethought. Since they are attractive only when in bloom, they are well suited among ground covers or in beds behind other low-growing plants. They will bloom reliably year after year and are surprisingly fragrant.

Last Frost Date

One of the most frequently asked questions of new gardeners is, "When can I plant things outside?" It's a valid question because even when starting seeds indoors they must be started in so-many days counted back from the last frost date. In Zone 6, planting can take place usually after May 15 without danger of those new plants being killed or damaged by frost. The average last frost date for Zone 6 is May 15. Even so, there may be an unusual cold snap after that date and covering your plants may be necessary. Today, with garden aids such as hot caps, Wall-O-waters and row covers, planting can be done successfully earlier than mid-May.

Many plants do not like cold soil, so will not put on new growth when soil temperatures are low. My own garden lies in a low, wet spot. Early gardening for me is not practical. Some garden sites are in a well-drained spot with a favorable southerly exposure. Gardening there can begin earlier.

When seedlings are ready for the garden, but then along comes a cold spell, it would be prudent to hold off planting until conditions improve.

Zone Map information is contained in every seed catalog and is a useful resource. Local agricultural extension offices will be glad to give this information, as well. Check the back of this book for details.

To Dig or Not to Dig?

Spring is here, so let's get things growing. If you haven't given much thought to the condition of your garden soil, now is the time. It is definitely worth planting your seeds and seedlings in a soil that is hospitable. Don't be too hasty with your garden work just yet. Working in the soil while it is still too wet will damage its tilth forever. It is too wet if a clump of it squeezed in your hand holds together like a big clod. Wait until the soil has become sufficiently dry so that it crumbles as it falls from your hand after being squeezed.

If your garden has become compacted in places, there is still hope. There's always room for additional soil improvement via addition of abundant amounts of organic matter -- manure, compost, sawdust, peat moss. Organic matter renders the soil finer-textured, softer and moisture retentive. That's just about ideal.

In much of Pennsylvania, soil is largely clay. Both clay and sandy conditions are corrected by addition of organics. With sandy soil, it takes lots more.

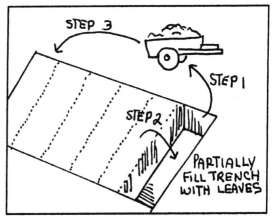

Garden beds generally should be loose to a depth of six to nine inches. If clay appears before reaching this depth, you have some choices:

1. One method is known as double digging. It's a lot of work but the results will be permanent and rewarding. Here's how. Dig a trench from one end of your plot straight to the other end, one foot wide and one foot deep. Store this soil in a barrow. Loosen the soil at the bottom by

forcing in a fork or shovel and wiggling it. Water it. Spread a layer of any organic material (such as leaves) over the loosened clumps at the bottom of the trench. Still with me?

Start digging a second trench one foot wide and one foot deep, right next to the first one, sliding that soil into the first trench. Repeat the breaking up of the subsoil with the fork, watering and adding a layer of organic material. Go on to the third one-foot row. At the end, fill the last trench with soil that was removed from the first. That was the hardest part. Now, spread more organic material over the whole bed and fork it in or use your garden rototiller.

2. Another method, recommended by a gardener friend, Betty Derbyshire, works well. Her method of conditioning heavy soil is to spread two to three inches of peat moss and two or three inches of construction sand on top of the bed and turn them in, mixing well. I used this method years ago. The soil is kept in good condition by regular additions of organics. Betty recommended construction sand because of its small pebbles, which contribute toward soil loosening.

3. One more choice is to make raised beds. Whole books have been written on this subject. Basically, the beds will be raised by means of mounding, or supported on each side by boards or logs, separated by pathways of dirt. Grass strips can be the separaters if you make the paths lawn-mower width in order to keep grass under control. Dirt pathways will sprout weeds which can be kept down by layers of straw or old carpeting. Plenty of organic material should be added to these beds which will raise the soil level in them. Each bed should be about 3 or 4 feet wide by whatever length you determine, such as 4 feet, 5, or 8, or 10 feet. (Read also *The Beauty of Raised Beds*, May.)

Now that the soil in your garden beds is loose and soft, none of these beds should ever be walked on. Compaction is not what you have done all this work for. If it is absolutely necessary to walk or step in a bed, lay a board down and step on it. Once garden soil has been conditioned and treated in any of these ways, it shouldn't have to be turned over or dug again. The only exception is when new compost is added once or twice each year. Now that the soil is ready, put in those seeds.

The Scoop on Fertilizers

Chemical Fertilizers: All plants are like hungry children, but what do we feed them, and when? Fertilizers come with three numbers on the package, such as 10-10-10 or 5-10-5. What does this mean? It means it takes more to grow plants than only soil, moisture and light. The three numbers on fertilizer packages represent major nutrients that are necessary for healthy plants. They are:

N - Nitrogen
P - Phosphorous
K - Potash or potassium

Most garden soils need a fertilizer that supplies these three ingredients. The numbers on the bags explain the percentage of nitrogen, phosphorous and potassium that the fertilizer contains. An example is a 10-10-10 formula contains 10% N, 10% P and 10% K.

N (nitrogen) is the element that gives a plant its dark green, healthy color. When nitrogen is added, a plant will put on a healthy growth spurt. Plants that need more of N are foliage plants.

P (phosphorous) helps build strong roots. It is easy to see that this is an important component. It is especially important to plants that are grown for their roots such as potatoes and carrots.

K (potash or potassium) helps the entire condition of a plant, helping it to bear fruit and resist disease.

In the spring it is a good idea to till or spade in an all-purpose fertilizer such as 10-10-10, working it evenly into the top two or three inches along with your compost or whatever other soil amendment you plan to add. Planting can now take place.

Fertilize again after plants have become established and once again as they begin to bloom. This is done by side dressing the plants. This means to apply a ring or band of commercial mix around each plant. Be sure to keep it no closer than four inches from the main stem. As a guide, approximately two cups of a dry fertilizer mix equals one pound.

Organic Fertilizers: Usually, organic fertilizers don't come in a bag or box from the store the way chemicals do. The price of organics can be very reasonable, or even free. We're talking about things like manures from farm animals, compost, decomposed hay and straw, crop residues, grass clippings and leaves.

When planning to use manure, there are a few things you should know first. Many manures are very strong and should not be used fresh. Fresh cow and horse manure should be aged about a year. If it's not possible to wait this long, it can be spread over the garden in the autumn and tilled into the soil in the spring. Winter snows and rains leach the nutrients into the soil beneath it, and by spring the soil will welcome the organic matter.

My grandfather gardened faithfully with a load of fresh cow manure dumped onto his garden every October. It lay on top all winter and was tilled in prior to spring planting. His garden was the best in town and he attributed it to the winter seasoning.

Chicken manure is very high in nitrogen and should be used sparingly. It should be aged 1 to 2 years. Too much of it or unaged will result in burned plants, or with very lush vegetation having very few fruits. If you do choose chicken manure (because it's available or free), age it, then sprinkle it lightly and work it well into the soil.

Compost is a great soil conditioner but is not regarded by many as a fertilizer. Most plants thrive on compost and an application of it may be all they need to do well. After several years of applying only compost to the garden, other soil deficiencies may develop. This can be remedied by adding fertilizers or the chemical or organic types.

A tremendous advantage of using organic fertilizers is that with each addition the soil structure is being improved, thereby increasing your chances of growing healthy plants of high production.

Regarding manure and compost: What if you have neither, but instead, you have quantities of grass clippings or old straw? It doesn't hurts to add too much of these organic materials to a garden, but while they decompose, they will be using up some of the nitrogen that is already present in the soil. These organic materials are best applied in the fall by tilling in. The nitrogen will gradually be replenished and if your spring crops show the slightest bit of nitrogen deprivation, shown by a sickly, yellowed appearance, this can quickly be remedied.

To be sure of your garden's chemical balance, use a soil test kit, obtained from a county Extension Agent (see *Don't Guess; Do a Soil Test*, November).

Of Weeds and Wildflowers
Coltsfoot

Coltsfoot (*Tussilago farfara*) is a little-known, ancient herb that, in April, makes its presence known by bright yellow, composite flowers on slim, scaly stalks about four to six inches high. It grows in full sun by roadsides or embankments. The yellow flower is easily mistaken for dandelion but there are no leaves present.

In a few short days, the flowers go to seed just like dandelions, making a white fluff. After going to seed, the leaves come up and are what gives the plant its name, round in the shape and the size of a colt's hoof.

Coltsfoot is a perennial that has a large network of roots. It is difficult to rid a garden of it once it invades. It is sometimes considered a ground cover and can be used as such.

For over 2,000 years it has been sought for its medicinal properties but modern science declares this plant an unsafe healer and a strongly suspected carcinogen.

On my property its rounded leaves grow up to 7 inches high in the summer but in the cooler climate and higher elevation of central Pennsylvania it reaches a height of over 12 inches. It can take over sunny areas at forest edges.

Throughout the centuries coltsfoot has been called coughwort. American Indians used it in a tea to relieve coughing that was made by boiling leaves, sweetened with honey or licorice. Vapors from a steaming pot of leaves were inhaled to remedy wheezing and asthma. In Scotland before matches were invented, scrapings of the fuzzy undersides of leaves were dried and used as tinder. The white fluff from faded flowers was used to stuff pillows.

Almost every plant that grows on this planet has been put to use as remedies for sickness and injury. It is simply astounding just how these plants came to be used in so many ways.

herb of the Month
Parsley

O ver the years I have experienced roaring successes with parsley, as well as many dismal failures. I think I have it all sorted out, for myself anyway, the best ways to bring each season's parsley to a happy conclusion.

Parsley is actually a full-sun biennial that, in our region, is handled as an annual.

Starting it by seed may be quite a challenge. The seeds are very tiny and have up to a three-week germination period. It is best to soak the seeds overnight before planting. Otherwise, growing parsley from seed is like any other -- using pre-moistened starter mix, keeping it evenly moist, and lots of light until the sprouts are ready to be hardened off.

> *"Harvest the more mature stems from the outside of the plant, leaving the younger, center ones to mature later."*

The best method for me, and one I recommend to others, is to buy started plants at the garden store. The hardest work is already done. Now comes the fun.

Parsley does best in loose soil of high organic matter. It develops tap roots, so if "containerizing" it in a pot, choose a pot not less than 12 inches deep. Several can grow in this size pot with a central plant of taller, upright stature such as dill or rosemary.

Provide all-purpose fertilizer for them in a liquid form or granular form. Another type that can be selected is the pelletized kind that will be mixed into the soil at the bottom of the hole and will gradually release nutrients for the whole season.

Keep the plants moist for the first several weeks until established, then taper off. Apply mulch around them about two to three inches deep.

During hot, dry spells of summer, water on a weekly basis if growing in the ground. Those in pots may need to be watered daily, as single pots dry out quickly.

In the early summer your parsley plants will start sending up flower stalks which can be cut off with a scissors.

Parsley can be harvested as soon as three sets of leaves have grown on the end of each stem. Harvest the more mature stems from the outer margins of the plant, leaving the younger, center ones to mature later. To create a bushier, rounder plant for better appearance in a container, remove the center leaf of each stem, leaving the two side ones in place.

In restaurants we see parsley added to salad platters which most people discard. But did you know it is a natural breath sweetener and digestive aid?

We all have recipes in which fresh, dried or frozen parsley can be used, but did you know of its medicinal benefits? Used for millennia, parsley tea has relieved many cases of rumbling, intestinal distress and was grown more for medicinal rather than culinary uses.

Several potted parsley plants can be brought into the house in the early autumn and used as a windowsill herb. One important note here is that it must have as much sun as possible in order for it to do well. It will be a welcome addition to cooking throughout the rest of the year and will contribute a healthy portion of vitamin C to your diet when you need it most.

> *Parsley can be "freeze-dried." Try this: Freeze sprigs in small amounts in air-tight plastic bags. Use as needed for any cooking. It will have the appearance of being fresh-picked.*

Removing the Mystery of Mulch

C ome green-up time, come weeds as well. One can't expect the good without the bad. But there are alternatives to this.

To avoid use of chemical weed controllers, one alternative is mulch. But it does much more than just control weeds. It also conserves moisture and keeps root zones cooler in hot weather. It protects the soil and plant roots against extreme temperature fluctuations, such as a few frosty nights, or a prolonged heat spell. By next year, or even autumn, it has started decomposing in place and adds that very important organic material to the soil. It keeps soil from splashing around in heavy rainstorms.

Mulch is simply ground-up organic material. It is bought by the scoopful, bagful or truck load from landscape nurseries. Usually a little coarse in nature, it allows the penetration of water to the soil below. It can be forked onto garden beds to about 2 or 3 inches deep. A mulch fork is useful for this task, or any other fork will do. Shovels are a little harder to force into the material but they work, too.

Weed seeds may still be there in your garden soil but the mulch prevents them from germinating. If they dare to sprout, they will likely be sparse, weak and spindly, and easy to pull out. Weeds that are spread by runners may be harder to control, but again, easier to remove once you observe that they are gaining purchase.

There are correct ways and incorrect ways to use mulch. In spreading it over garden soil, keep it several inches away from the stems of your plants. Apply it when the soil is still moist, as in the spring. If applied over dry soil, it will serve only to keep the soil beneath it too dry.

Used in a band of several feet in diameter around tree trunks, it helps avoid trunk damage by lawn mowers or string weed cutters. Again, keep the mulch away from the trunk by several inches, graduating its depth. We have all seen mulch beds around landscape trees that are piled high up the tree's trunk like a volcano. That's a bad example of application, for if applied deeply enough against the tree's bark, it can cause sprouts, make a place for insects to enter the tree or mice to girdle the tree.

Mulch is usually applied in the spring to dress garden beds after planting. It can be applied again in the fall to prevent frost heaving.

During the summer, tree trimming companies that prune trees for utility lines may come through neighborhoods. They trail a branch shredder with them and make tons of chips in a day's time which they give away free to anyone who asks. This is fine material to use in home gardens but a caution should be mentioned. If you know roughly what trees have been chipped in the free load you will receive, well and good, but if not, be cautious. The load may contain chips from black walnut trees that are toxic to many garden plants. They may also include tough vines of poison ivy or diseased trees.

If you know your street or neighborhood you can guess closely whether the load of chips is what you want. However, because it is green wood and includes leaves, it should be stored in an out-of-the-way corner of your property to age for several months.

Good and bad examples of applying mulch.

On Keeping a Garden Journal

It's planting time. Let's see. What did I grow last year? How many plants did I put in? Were the beds too crowded? Did we like the Romano beans or not? I don't remember if we liked the variety of peppers. What were those little red ones? I think I bought the pink begonias with bronze leaves; or were they red with bronze? What were those tomatoes that did so well -- or did so poorly? Don't remember the dates when I planted outside; was it the middle of May, or the end? What did I use this insecticide for last year? When did I start the seeds inside?

Questions like these can go through your mind like a frenzy at planting time and you may never recall the answers -- *unless* you kept a garden journal to jot down all those things that puzzle you now.

A garden journal can be a very fancy book or very utilitarian in which you record all kinds of details. It can be a tablet from the store, a school composition notebook or the "freebie" calendar from the supermarket -- anything that is comfortable in which to keep track of all those things you need to know *now*. Memory lapse has happened to me. You think you wouldn't possibly forget, but you do. I grew snapdragons one year that were perfect. Got them from a seed catalog but I tossed away the package. Mistake. If I'd recorded it in my journal, I'd know today where to find more just like them.

The journal is very useful to jot down dates of planting, both indoors and out, weather patterns of frost or drought, fertilizing schedules and insects that mysteriously appeared and how they were dealt with. And more!

How many bags of manure, topsoil or mulch were bought and what were the prices of them? How many onions were put in? What was the cost of the entire garden for that year?

Once you start making notes -- not fancy, mind you -- you will refer to them again and again. The uncertain feeling that each year is just another experiment will fade away. Now you have all those important details in black and white and finally you know what you're doing.

And spelling doesn't count.

Beating Diseases

Make it a practice to read the information on seed packets or nursery plant tabs when shopping. Vegetables such as cucumbers, melons, tomatoes, peppers, eggplants are susceptible to two fungal diseases -- fusarium and verticillium wilt. If those soil-borne diseases are present in your garden, the plants mentioned may not make it to maturity. Another one that can be troublesome is root knot nematodes.

Early in my gardening experience, I lost all my cucumbers and gourds. At the same time, my tomatoes were dying of fusarium and verticillium wilts. By mid-July my garden was a disaster.

The wilts start with whole branches suddenly collapsing, and with yellowed leaves turning brown and dying. Once plants are affected, there is no cure. Just remove and destroy.

Nematodes are tiny worms that create scars and galls on roots that promote rotting and stunting. The plants mentioned above plus corn, onions and lettuce are susceptible.

The best protection is built-in resistance, thanks to today's plant breeders. Look on seed packages or plant tags for information such as "Disease Resistant" or VF or VFN. The letters VF indicate resistance to verticillium and fusarium wilts. The N describes resistance to root knot nematodes. If not shown on the front of the package, it may be listed on the back. If not mentioned at all, I would avoid that variety if you know these disease conditions exist in your garden.

When these diseases go through your garden, remove and destroy all affected plants immediately. The soil will be contaminated, but next year you can choose a disease-resistant crop or a crop not susceptible. Save yourself some trouble, though, and buy the resistant varieties.

Other things to look for are CMV (cucumber mosaic virus), MV (mosaic virus), PV (potato virus), PM (powdery mildew).

Spraying against aphids and leafhoppers helps, for they spread viruses. Stay out of your garden when leaves are wet, for that will spread fungus and mold diseases you'd rather not have.

Avoid smoking cigarettes in the garden. Some plants are affected by tobacco mosaic virus which can be transferred via cigarettes.

Lettuce Culture

One of the best spring vegetables that can help break through to spring once and for all is lettuce. It thrives in cool weather and will be ready to harvest in 6 weeks. A planting right now, if your garden soil is not too wet, will be ready for your salads in early June. Head lettuces take 9 or 10 weeks, so if you're looking for an earlier harvest, use the loose leaf varieties. Seeds germinate at 60 degrees but when temperatures reach a fairly consistent 80 degrees or more, plants will bolt and become bitter-tasting. Seeds can again be planted in late summer when temperatures moderate. If seeds are not your specialty, started plants in market packs are very reliable.

Lettuce thrives in soil that is high in organic matter.

Red Sails has been a winner in our garden. Green Ice seems extra crisp and juicy. Some seed companies offer packets in a gourmet blend. Try this to experiment with different varieties.

Other longer-season crops, such as peppers or cabbages, can be interplanted with the loose leaf lettuces. You will find that lettuce-growing will come to an end as hot weather develops and that is when the long-season crops will need the extra space.

The lettuce season can be extended by covering plants with shade cloth to keep them cooler. After harvesting, rinse and store it in a closed plastic bag in the refrigerator.

Very few diseases or insects affect lettuce. However, slugs can be a menace. Many slug control methods are known through what we call the "garden grapevine" (tested by gardeners, that is) but not very scholarly or scientific.

Slugs: I stopped a lot of them dead in their tracks one year with saucers of beer in the garden but it took a lot of beer. Another method is to hunt them at night with a flashlight and hand pick them (ugh). Or salt them down with a shaker. Trap them under boards laid in the garden overnight. Spread a light band of wood ashes around plants that need protection. While these methods work, slugs sometimes reproduce faster than they can be disposed of using these techniques. The garden store will have slug remedies that will work wonders. The choice is up to you.

Full of Beans

For those who still grow the standard Blue Lake variety of bush bean, sit up and take notice. There is lots to learn.

Bush snap beans bear heavily and are worth the space in your garden. My neighbors tell me that pole beans yield more than bush and you don't have to bend over to pick them. When I tried Kentucky Wonder Pole beans for the first time I found them to be just great.

The Scarlet Runner pole bean has been around forever. It blooms with red flowers until frost. Because of its ornamental quality it doesn't *have* to be in the vegetable patch. But it does provide good eating-quality beans if picked young.

Asparagus, the novelty-type pole bean, grows beans long enough that 2 or 3 make a single serving. These are fun, but they definitely lack flavor. Because they are so slim it is difficult to judge maturity.

Espada is an excellent bush bean, maturing sooner and bearing a few weeks longer than standards. The secret is to keep them well-picked to encourage blossoming -- every day or two.

Royal Burgundy or purple beans are eye catchers, producing extremely well, but when cooked, may turn green, making the purple color irrelevant. Some cooked ones seem to be a little fuzzy. You may find other purple varieties less fuzzy. Don't pass these by completely, for their beauty lies in using fresh on raw vegetable plates and in salads.

Wax Romano is a bright yellow, flat Italian style. It is excellent, mild in taste, great with any meal or for freezing. This is high on my list of preferred garden beans.

When shopping for seeds read the packages carefully to make sure you get what you want and find out what disease resistance is bred in.

While I recommend frequent picking -- every 1 or 2 days -- be careful not to do this when leaves are wet. Just brushing against them or each other can introduce a fungus disease that will ruin your growing efforts.

As with most vegetables, beans do best in full sun and are relatively drought tolerant. They respond well with even watering, especially during flowering time and pod-set time. They should produce for the whole summer.

After harvesting, refrigerate in a closed plastic bag until needed.

Transplanting A, B, Cs

There is nothing mysterious about transplanting, but there are a few basic rules to be aware of for the best results.

A. Transplant bedding plants and seedlings on an overcast day or late afternoon, avoiding the strongest sun rays. If the sun is hot for the next few days, shade the transplants.

B. Water the plants before taking them out of their original containers to prevent drying of the tiny roothairs as the transfer is made. That water should be from a bucket that has warmed a bit in the sun. I usually submerge the pots, plants and all, for a few minutes in the bucket. In transferring plants to their permanent home, use as much of the potted soil as possible. Small market-pack plants are usually well-rooted and the entire rootball is easily removed in one piece. This may not be so with larger, potted perennials. Water well for a few days thereafter, gradually tapering off until they have become established. Peat pots should be thoroughly saturated before planting so as not to draw moisture from the plant itself.

C. Handle seedlings with extreme care. In removing them from pots, don't tug on the stem or leaf-tops. Tissues will be damaged that way. Instead, run a knife blade around the inside of the pot to loosen the plant before extracting it.

D. Prepare a hole to receive the plant, set the plant in at its proper depth, and fill back with soil that has been mixed with compost. Tamp in place gently with fingers to remove air pockets. Add water and press the soil around the plant lightly to make sure of removing any remaining air pockets.

E. Sometimes it is puzzling just how deep to plant. Most plants need to be put in at the same depth they were in their pots. However, there are always exceptions to any rule. Cabbages, melons, zucchini and cucumbers can be set about an inch deeper than they were in their pots. For tomatoes, eggplants and peppers, bury the stems *and* the first set of leaves. This procedure allows roots to form along the buried stems, creating much stronger plants.

F. Spread mulch around the plants after settling them into the ground, remembering to keep it back a few inches from each stem.

Insect Insights
Japanese Beetles

Those bronze-metallic-colored beetles about ½ inch long that are seen clinging to leaves and each other every summer are Japanese beetles. They were the first garden insects we were introduced to as kids. Because they were larger than a lot of insects, they were easy to grasp in the fingers and drop in a can of soapy water. When we were on Beetle Patrol, we skulked around the grapevines and roses grasping at every beetle we could reach. Their feet were kind of stickery and we didn't like that, but they could be brushed off the leaves into the can without too much of a struggle.

Japanese beetles are seen in the eastern half of the United States to the Mississippi River. Their appetites include many vegetables as well as flowers and ornamentals.

During the day they feed on plants in the full sun. They virtually skeletonize leaves in their feasting. They also chew on flowers, causing them to wilt and die. At the end of summer, the beetles burrow under the grass and lay their eggs.

These eggs hatch into larvae which feed on the grass. The grubs (larvae stage) are white with a yellow or brown head and are curled into a C shape. Their bodies are about 3/4 inch long. When cold weather comes, they burrow several inches into the soil to lie dormant until spring, when they move closer to the soil surface to feed on grass roots, go through a brief pupate period then emerge as adults in mid-summer to start eating again.

Often, when there is a mole problem in a lawn, it is related to the Japanese beetle grubs which they eat, damaging your lawn to do so.

As described above, the best method of control is hand-collecting, If you don't mind pulling them into your hand-held vacuum cleaner, that is another option. Otherwise beetle traps may work if everyone in the neighborhood uses them. One trap in one yard will not control a population of beetles in a whole neighborhood. Milky spore disease (*Bacillus popilliae*) can be used on the lawn to kill larvae.

Rainy Day Quiz

Test your knowledge of these very important things that you never knew you needed to know.

1. When cutting blossoms for indoors, why cut the stems on the slant?

2. What is the national flower?

3. What decorative vine can also be used as a vegetable source?

4. What "peculiarity" do all members of the mint family share?

5. What good are wood ashes to a garden?

Answers

1. Cut blossom stems on a slant to allow more surface area to absorb water. It also prevents stems from standing flush on the bottom of the vase preventing any water absorption at all.

2. Rose.

3. Scarlet Runner Bean (*Phaseolus coccineus*). It continues to bloom with flowers of scarlet red if beans are picked often.

4. They all have square stems.

5. It can be used in a sprinkled band around plants to prevent invasions of slugs and other soft-bodied insects. Also, it can be added to the compost pile, but only in small, occasional doses.

Checklist

✔Removing generous sprays of lilacs for cut flowers won't hurt the bush, but keep in mind the shape of the bush while doing so.

✔Support your local plants! Good materials to use for tying them to stakes are torn or cut strips of old T-shirts and legs of old pantyhose -- all soft but strong.

✔Peonies can get heavy blossoms, especially when rain water loads them up. Keep them off the ground by using wire rings or use stakes with soft fabric to encircle the plants. Irises also benefit from being supported, for they too can become rain-laden and may fall over.

✔It is time to fill window boxes and hanging baskets with annuals. Mulch them to conserve moisture throughout the growing season and remember that containers of any kind dry out much sooner than garden beds do.

✔Pinch off the top two inches of upright chrysanthemum stems this month. Repeat a pinching-off when the shoots grow another six inches. Keep pruning routinely in July. After this, flower buds start forming and by then you should have a good, compact plant.

✔A good addition to potting soil is crushed eggshells. They promote better drainage, add calcium to the soil and make it a little more alkaline.

✔Poison ivy may be a scourge in some yards. It used to be in mine. Wait until there is a good, soaking rain then go out with plastic bags rubber-banded to your hands and a trash bag. The roots come right out of the loose soil. Pop them into the bag and put it all in the trash.

✔The end of May opens the picnic season. Grow a good crop of basil. Reason: At any of your outdoor picnics you can repel flies by using bouquets of basil or having several pots of it on tables (see *Herb of the Month, Basil,* May).

✔The daffodil season is over and was beautiful while it lasted. What should be done with leaves that are in the way? Some gardeners tie them up in knots; others fold them over and tie with rubber bands. Foliage dies back in July. (See *Spring Bulbs,* October.)

✔Hummingbirds return to this region on May 1. Invite them and the butterflies to your garden. Grow bee balm, columbines, begonias, nasturtiums, impatiens, geraniums, phlox and vines such as morning glory, trumpet and scarlet runner bean. Feeders are fun to mount near a window to see these birds in action.

✔In May we may still get light frosts. Plants already set out won't mind being cool; the cold will just slow their growth. But they don't like frost damage. To prevent this, use hot caps but be aware that when the sun hits them they can overheat. Paper milk cartons are good with the tops cut off and the bottoms sliced around 3 sides. Slip them over the plants with the bottom flap open for warmth, and shut in case of overnight frost.

✔Good free mulch is available every time the grass gets cut. Let clippings dry a day or two in the sun, then layer them on the soil around your plants, not letting them touch the plant stems directly. Do not use clippings from a chemically-treated lawn or those which may contain weed seeds.

✔ Make a delicious herb butter with fresh rosemary leaves from your garden. Use 6 tablespoons softened butter and 2 teaspoons of finely chopped, fresh rosemary. Mix thoroughly and refrigerate.

✔ I have it on good authority that if planting one onion set between seed potatoes, potato bugs will shy away from your potato patch.

> *Hummingbird nectar: Add ½ cup of sugar to 2 cups of water. Cook just to boiling, set aside and cool. Do not add food coloring. Replace every week, or more often.*

Repotting houseplants

I f you like your houseplants to be outside for the summer, late May is a good time to move them. They will flourish outside and be beautiful in September when it's time for them to come in. Some gardeners prefer not to keep them outside for the summer because of insects that would be brought into the house (see *Insect Insights*, March).

Even if they do not take that summer vacation outdoors, they may need to be repotted. Take a critical look at them. Most will benefit from repotting every few years. The best time is in the spring when the shock of repotting can be offset by several months of long days and ideal weather.

How do you know when they have outgrown their living quarters? If you knock the plant out of its pot and observe that its hairlike roots can be seen on the outside of the "earth ball," it is time to repot.

Use a pot that is only one size larger. Place a pottery shard, stone or a few small pieces of torn newspaper over the hole. Sift in some new potting soil. You can use a purchased mix or, if you prefer, create your own. Use this formula: Equal parts of compost, peat moss and vermiculite. Put several inches of soil in the pot. Hold the plant in the pot and add more of your mixture around its sides, poking it down with a ruler or paint stick. The soil level should be about one inch below rim of the pot. That's all it takes.

Start with the largest plants first, shifting them to new, larger pots. Then work downward in size, using the newly emptied ones. However, first, submerge the empty pots into a bucket of water-and-bleach solution (9 parts water/1 part bleach), scrub and rinse well before reusing.

Note that I suggest repotting into pots of only one size larger. There's a good reason for this. If the pot is too big, you will have a small plant in a big pot with unneeded amounts of soil and water. This can seriously cause a set back in top growth while root growth continues. The best policy is to plan on investing a little money on inexpensive pots of the right size if you do not have them in stock at home. This allows the opportunity to buy ones that are sculptured or otherwise eye-appealing.

hardening Off

As promised in the March chapter, *Seed Starting Made Easy*, we go now to the next step in getting those tender seedlings ready for the great outdoors, preparing them for the shock of living with wind, sun and colder air after being tended in your seedling nursery. It can be a time when some fatalities occur, but don't be discouraged. I haven't lost any yet so you can stay hopeful.

Begin withholding water for about 2 days before taking them outside. Leave them out for only a few hours the first day in a partially shaded place. If it's windy, protect them from that by choosing a sheltered spot. Extend the hours each day, bringing them inside each time. The process will take about a week or two. Check for dryness and sudden weather changes. Fertilize again for the final transplanting, and put them into the ground only as deep as their own soil level is.

For tomatoes, eggplants and peppers, put them in up to the first set of leaves. Roots will develop along the length of the buried (planted!) stem, strengthening the plant considerably.

Tricks to Try

Tricks are learned from gardening experiences year after year that make the growing job easier.

Some seeds that will be direct-sown may be very fine such as carrots or lettuce, so it can be difficult to distribute them evenly. Half-fill a cup with soil and mix in the quantity of seeds you plan to sow. There is now enough volume to sprinkle uniformly. I've used this many times.

If you've had cutworms before, be prepared for them again. When putting your transplants out, surround each stem with a collar of stiff paper, such as the upper portion of a paper cup. Push the collar into the ground as well as leaving a rim of an inch or two above the soil.

Another cutworm preventive would be to use a two-inch band (lightly applied) of wood ashes around each stem. The collars and wood-ash bands will also deter slimy slugs.

Shady herbs

Would you love to grow some herbs but don't have enough sun in your garden to do so? Most annuals and perennials have full-sun requirements, meaning they need 6 or more hours of sunlight daily to do their best. For shady yards, planting full-sun plants doesn't make sense. Do not despair if you think that shady spots must be relegated to grass only. There are some interesting and useful herbs that will tolerate shady places.

Mints are usually thought of as full-sun plants, but it may surprise you to learn that they will do well under tall trees and in partial shade. All members of the mint family have square stems, but the plants vary in shape, height, in flowers and fragrance. The mint called lemon balm grows about two feet tall and in late summer produces small white or yellow flowers. A variegated lemon balm is attractive in an otherwise green setting. (See *Herb of the Month*, February.)

Bee balm, also known as *Monarda*, Bergamot and Oswego Tea can grow several feet tall, bearing bright blooms in mid-summer. Its leaves impart a minty fragrance and the flowers attract bees as well as hummingbirds. It is the flavoring ingredient in Earl Grey tea.

There are other mints, such as spearmint, peppermint, curley mint, woolly mint and catnip, all of which made delicious teas or flavorings.

Tarragon, which is not a mint, can be considered for a location in part-shade and of course can be dried or used fresh in recipes.

Sweet woodruff is a ground cover with whorls of pointed leaves around the stems, blooming with little white blossoms in May and June. This low-growing herb is used as flavoring in German May wines and gives off a hay-scent with a hint of vanilla.

Borage is a good candidate for some shade. Its young leaves can be used in salads and lemonade. It has pretty blue flowers that, for the herb collector, can be candied.

My comfrey plant is hale and hearty growing under an oak tree on the north side of the house. (see *Herb of the Month*, June.)

All these can be grown from seed, but bedding plants will give very rewarding results.

Insect Insights
Tent Caterpillars

Eastern tent caterpillars are noticeable this time of year because of white, webby nests that they build at the crotches of tree and shrub branches.

The female moth (about 1 to 1 ½ inch wingspan, striped, brownish in color) lays eggs mid-summer. The brown egg masses look like stiff foam plastic wrapped around stems and twigs about the size of a chewing gum wad. Tent caterpillars particularly like fruit trees and some sweet shrubs, so that is where eggs are likely to be laid. Small fruit trees can be seriously defoliated by these voracious insects.

When they hatch in the spring, the larvae move to the nearest crotch on their branch and start spinning webs around themselves. From this nest they explore for nearby leaves to consume, for now they have huge appetites. While small, damage can be light, but as they increase in size the damage in defoliation to fruit trees and shrubs can be enormous, especially in a high-population year.

They emerge from their tents at night to feed on tender, green leaves and come back to the nests at dawn. As they get older, they stay out day and night to continue eating

At one time, it was a common practice to tie rags around the end of a long pole, soak them with gasoline and ignited to burn away the tents. But this damaged the trees as well.

Inspection during the winter of susceptible trees will reveal the egg masses. Cut, or rub them off. When nests form, they, too, can be destroyed by hand. When infestations are not severe, perhaps they can be left alone, for other natural insects will prey on them. In high-infestation years, control is recommended. Young, or dwarf trees can survive an occasional defoliation and will resprout in several weeks, but repeated defoliations weaken them to other diseases and insects.

Strawberry Jars

Strawberry jars make nice gifts for occasions such as Mother's Day, especially when planted with herbs. If Mom is still active in the kitchen, this can be fun for her to receive and use. But if herbs will not be your preference in such a container, try flowers like impatiens, portulacas and any other small flower varieties.

These special pots are available in every garden store. They are usually tall, red clay, urn-shaped pots with staggered openings in the sides to accommodate the insertion of small plants. As the plants mature, they grow as they would from the face of a stone wall, trailing or blooming attractively. They are usually sold empty, but sometimes already pre-planted.

It is not hard to plant your own. All you need is the jar, gravel or pebbles, the tube from paper towel roll (or two taped together end to end), pre-moistened potting soil, an assortment of plants.

Fill the bottom two inches of the jar with gravel. Stand the cardboard tube inside and fill the tube with the gravel or pebbles. Then start filling the jar around the tube with potting soil. As the level of soil rises to the side holes, insert the new plants and keep filling with soil around the tube. When nearly at the top, carefully pull out the tube and plant the rest of the selection in the top. The gravel core helps to distribute water to the interior and lower half of the jar, keeping its contents from becoming too dry.

> *When using a clay pot for a container garden, thoroughly soak the empty pot before starting. Then the clay will not take up the water that is meant for the soil.*

An alternative to the removable cardboard tube is a length of PVC pipe the same height as the jar with a number of ½-inch holes drilled through it intermittently along its length. Fill the pipe with quick-draining pebbles or small gravel. The pipe will remain in the jar and watering will be done by filling the pipe, filtering out the holes, keeping the soil evenly moist.

herb of the Month
Basil

May is a good time to start basil (*Ocimum basilicum*). The seeds germinate in about 5 to 10 days. It is a full-sun annual. There is a wide range of basils to please you. In reviewing seed catalogs, you will find some very common ones and some very different ones. There's lemon flavored, anise and cinnamon, lettuce-leaf type, Green Ruffles and Purple Ruffles. There is also Dark Opal and just plain sweet basil. The list goes on and on.

This herb is an old one and is known world-wide. In this region, early Pennsylvania Germans called it *Fersomlingshaus Graut* (Meetinghouse herb) because its spicy, scented leaves served as a perfume in crowded meeting houses during the hot summer months.

Dark Opal has leaves of mahogany color and is used fresh in salads, sandwiches and snipped over sliced tomatoes. Purple Ruffles has the same uses; however, in growing, it tends to be dwarfish and somewhat finicky. Many of these dark basils look wonderful when included in summer flower arrangements.

Green Ruffles has the same uses as its cousin, Purple, and has the same growing habits.

Cinnamon basil is a delicious addition to baked apples. Sprinkle a few leaves over the tops of the apples while baking, and serve with a fresh sprig or two. Use whenever a touch of cinnamon is desired. Its leaves also make a comforting hot tea drink, when used with a little honey.

Don't neglect to include sweet basil in your garden. It is a standard, is easily grown and rarely disappointing. It is a must with all tomato dishes.

Virtually any variety of basil is excellent in salads, soups and fish dishes. Try steeping sprigs in white vinegar for a flavorful salad dressing. Purple basils make a pleasing pink vinegar. In the garden, it can be interplanted with tomatoes, its strong scent often acting as a pest repellant.

Apply a high nitrogen fertilizer for foliage growth. Sometimes slugs or Japanese beetles are a problem but they can easily be picked off (for slug remedies, see *Lettuce Culture*, April).

Get a Good Garden Buy

By now garden beds are raked and ready for the annual bedding plants, just as an artist's blank canvas is ready for a colorful painting. What comes next is to choose and buy the plants. Seeds of annual bedding plants have been started in a greenhouse from 6 weeks to 3 months ago and will flower almost instantly, compared to those that you direct-seed at home. So with nursery bedding plants, you're off to a fast start of blooms all summer.

Many plants will be available from which to choose your favorites. Avoid buying those already in full bloom. These will take longer to become established than younger ones that are still in bud.

Check the leaves. Select only those with a good green color. Also look for compact growth, avoiding ones that are tall and leggy.

If trying new varieties and you are unsure of suitability, get advice from the label, a clerk or consult a garden catalog at home.

Watch for whiteflies and other insects when shopping. If there are any present at all, shop elsewhere.

It also helps to shop early. There are those annuals that are everyone's favorite -- white impatiens, for example -- which may be gone if you want that color and wait too long.

If the plants you see are not blooming yet, depend on the plant marker for color information and disease resistance. When you see what you want, don't procrastinate. Get it.

There are one or two more tips for transferring to the garden.

Try to plant your purchased seedlings the same day they are bought. But if that is not possible, place them where they will get good light (not in a dark garage) and keep them watered. Prepare holes for them. Dip the market packs into a bucket of water to thoroughly saturate; then drain. Run a knife blade around the inside edges of the market pack and gently lift each plant out. Press into the soil at exactly the same depth as in the original container (except for tomatoes, eggplants and peppers -- they can go deeper). Never leave a plant out of its container for more than a few seconds. Those nearly-invisible root hairs can suddenly dry out, causing a set-back to occur.

Water them in and you've earned a rest and glass of iced tea.

Fruit Trees in Your Yard

I n a few short weeks you will be able to see that your fruit trees have set their bounty and that they are getting larger by the day.

It may be a good idea to thin some clusters. This will promote better quality to those that remain.

For apples, thin to one or two apples per cluster. This thinning can be done before the natural apple-drop occurs. It prevents crowding and will produce larger fruit.

Use pointed scissors to remove any misshapen ones that are obviously not perfect. Do not pull them off by hand as this is likely to damage the spur.

Seckel pears may also need thinning.

It's a good idea to keep a ring of mulch around the base of fruit trees. This is not "just for pretty." It will prevent bumping and nicks from lawn mowers or string trimmers. Those nicks in the bark produce the ideal spot for borers to enter and do their damage.

Another way to prevent borers is to push the soil away from the base of the trunk about 2 or 3 inches down and start wrapping the trunk with masking tape. Wrap it upward several inches and replace the soil. The tape will help prevent borers from attacking for several years. The tape will split as the tree grows and will cause no problems.

What happens if the damage has already started? Symptoms include a gummy ooze that will be seen near the base of the tree, and there may be wilting or dying branches above. Probe the hole of entry with a thin, flexible wire.

A remedy for wintertime nibbling of tree trunks by small rodents like hungry rabbits or mice who burrow under the snow, is to wrap the tree trunk with 1/4 inch hardware mesh from just below the soil surface to a height of several feet. Garden stores also carry a tree-wrap product which is very good to use.

Remember, diligence and watchfulness can catch small problems before they become major ones. That ounce of prevention is worth a pound of cure.

Squash -- Summer, Winter
What's the Difference?

Summer versus winter squash -- can we grow both? Of course! We can and do. The tender summer ones are those like zucchini and yellow squash. They can be eaten fresh or frozen in casseroles. Winter squash, like butternut, acorn, Hubbard, spaghetti squash and pumpkin mature more slowly, taking almost twice as long as summer varieties. They form a hard skin and can be stored for several months for sweet, nutritious fall and winter eating.

Despite the differences in both taste and appearance, summer and winter are closely related botanically and are cultivated in the same way. They belong to the gourd family, along with cucumbers and melons. All of them need lots of space to grow but some bush varieties can do nicely for you in the smaller garden or in a container. They all need moist, rich soil and do their best when fertilized.

Seeds can be planted outdoors (direct-seeded) about the same time that tomato and eggplant seedlings are put out. That would be in May when night temperatures stay above 55 degrees.

They can also be started indoors but will not transplant well if the roots are disturbed. Unless you are able to start them in something no smaller than a 3-inch peat pot, do not attempt it. Certainly, do not expect success in transplanting squash seedlings if there are any roots coming through the pots.

They are subject to a considerable number of pests and diseases but diligence on the gardener's part always pays dividends.

Striped cucumber beetles can spread a bacterial disease that causes plants to wilt and die. Using row covers for the first several weeks will cut down on the problem.

Squash vine borers tunnel through the plant's stalk after they have hatched from eggs in the soil. If you see borers are already at work, they can be cut out with a knife if caught early enough the plant will survive.

Fusarium wilt is a fungus (for which there is no cure), and powdery mildew (see *Beating Diseases*, April) are the ones to watch for. Always read the information on seed packets that will tell you what diseases those seeds are bred to resist.

The Beauty of Raised Beds

L ong ago I planted my gardens in single, marching rows just like everyone else in the neighborhood did, but in reading up on the subject, I came to realize that one of the best arrangements for gardens is raised beds.

The raised bed concept is not a new one. It actually goes back thousands of years and was used as a garden method in parts of the world where poor soil or bad weather conditions existed. It came to America from Europe with the first settlers and its success is still appreciated today. Raised beds are perfect for an area, for instance, that is low-lying where lingering puddles of rain contribute to compaction of soil, leave the soil wet until late in the season and cause plants to stand with wet feet.

Raised beds are usually supported on four sides by boards; for instance, in 4-foot by 4-foot sections, or 4-foot by 6- or 8-foot sections. The walkways between, about 2 feet wide, or lawn-mower width, would give adequate foot and kneeling room. But any size bed is up to you, the gardener -- just so long as you can reach from the path into the center of each bed. (See *To Dig or Not to Dig,* April.)

These beds have the same advantages as wide rows because in a sense, the wide rows become raised partly due to the soil amendments and conditioners that have been added, plus the fact that no compaction occurs from footsteps or from standing puddles of rain. Therefore, the soil in which plants grow stays light and aerated.

Other advantages are that the beds warm earlier and drain earlier in the spring, giving a slight head start to planting.

Calculating quantities of fertilizer becomes easier when the gardener already knows exactly how many square feet are within the frames.

I would suggest some tilling before setting up the frames, made of 1X4s or 2X4s, and staked in place. When the boards are in place, your choice of soil is ready to be added. Adding new soil is another advantage because a much better quality of soil can be used than what might already lie beneath. Wide beds stay uniformly moist, compared to the older-style of single rows that are isolated from each other.

Give raised beds a try. I can almost guarantee you'll like it.

Soil ph

Hydrochloric acid	Lemons Vinegar	Grapefruit	Boric Acid	Manure Sea Water	Ammonia Washing Soda	Lye

0	1	2	3	4	5	6	7	8	9	10	11	12	13	14

I s your garden soil acid or alkaline? This is measured on the pH scale, shown above, which goes from 0 (pure acid) to 14 (pure lye or alkaline.)

Why does it matter? The answer is, because most plants, flowers and vegetables, for instance, do very well when the soil acid ranges toward the middle of the scale, or neutral -- about 6 to 7 pH. But other plants, such as hollies and evergreens, do better in a slightly more acid soil.

Knowing the pH of your soil makes it easier for you to know what corrections are to be made to allow plants in your particular yard to do their best for you. It may not matter what variety vegetable is grown, but if the pH is correct, the quality of that plant should be superior.

A simple soil pH home test kit may be bought in many garden centers. Through your local Cooperative Extension Service, listed in the back of this book, a soil test kit may be obtained for which you will supply a soil sample. The result of this will be more complete than just providing the pH reading and it will inform you what else is necessary to correct any other soil deficiencies there may be. More complete information on soil testing is found in *Don't Guess; Do a Soil Test*, November.

Of Weeds and Wildflowers
Forget-me-nots

Forget-me-nots (*Myosotis*) are among those flowers that moved from gardens to meadows and damp marshes. The clustered blossoms are bright sky blue and display themselves in profusion, catching the eye wherever they are. They are listed in some catalogs as biennial and annual, depending on the species.

Only several inches high, they are more than suitable for rock gardens and filling in around perennials and borders. Light requirement for them is sun to shade. Their bloom period is several weeks long in the spring and into early summer. As the blossoms die, seed pods form and they may, at this stage, look rather sad and shaggy. I always choose a few particular ones to let stay in place until the seeds ripen. Then I scatter the dried seeds into beds where I would like to see them next year to ensure their continued presence. I discard many of the plants after seed production. Whether annual or biennial, self-seeding has kept them growing in my garden for more than 15 years.

Leaves stay green virtually all summer in compact little bunches, so the only time they may be unattractive is during the seed production time.

Although not classified as an evergreen, in my garden their small clusters of leaves can still be found throughout the winter. These little wildflower gems never disappoint, stepping in after the daffodils have finished. They put on a lovely appearance when interplanted with tulips.

For some reason, their self-sown seeds like my gravel path and if I do not remove most of the volunteers there, visitors hesitate to tread on them, and have to pick their way along to avoid stepping on the flowers. Forget-me-nots do not require special soil, although if your beds are amended with organic materials, they will not falter.

Big Blooms--hydrangeas

Not much ado is made about hydrangeas. They seem to be taken for granted in many landscapes and are very under-appreciated. They are one of the showiest shrubs to be seen in the American garden, producing flowers from early spring to early fall. Depending on which type, they can be deciduous or evergreen, and are really a cinch to take care of. They do well in full sun but just as well in partial/light shade.

There are many types of hydrangeas; one is known as *H.macrophylla*, or hortensia or French hydrangea, or bigleaf. It has large, round mopheads of flowers in pink or blue and are usually the common ones seen potted in spring garden store displays. This type offers a variety called Lace Cap that has flat, lacey blossoms that are very pretty in blues or whites. The Peegee (*H paniculata grandiflora*) often reaches 25 feet in height, blooms through August and September with very large, pyramidal heads of white flowers sometimes tinged with light pink or pale green. Dried, the heads are effective in flower arrangements and dry wreaths. It's a great shrub to have when there is not much else blooming in August but because of its large stature, is best-proportioned to a medium or large-sized yard. Then there is the oak-leaf variety with large white blossoms and lobed leaves resembling red oak foliage. When growing in a sunny spot, its foliage will become a rose-maroon in the fall, making it a focal point in the autumn as well as summer. So you see, there are quite a few choices to make when shopping.

Any of these hydrangeas will look handsome in a bed of ground cover such as pachysandra, periwinkle or ivy. These ground covers are invasive, but they do have their place in the garden if they don't spill over their bounds.

When planting hydrangeas in the spring or fall, add only a moderate amount of well-composted material and make sure they are mulched. They like moisture, as the name implies, so keep them well-watered in summer dry spells.

See instructions for a dried hydrangea wreath in *Checklist* for September.

Blueberries for You

If looking for small bushes for the yard that will be all of these things -- a native plant, pest and disease free, hardy in the coldest of winters, unharmed by late frosts, small enough for easy pruning, big enough to discourage weeds, colorful in the fall, and bears fruit -- blueberries are the choice.

Their requirements are fairly simple. Plant them in lots of organic matter, surrounded by lots of mulch and give them lots of water to drink. Add to that an annual pruning. That's not a lot to ask in exchange for a full month of berry harvest.

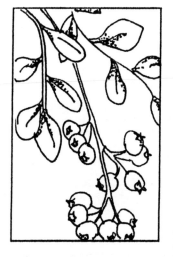

They are not very demanding, except when it comes time to plant. Care should be taken to do it right the first time. For this, they will show their appreciation.

Blueberries will tolerate living in an acid clay but why let them do that when they will flourish in an acid soil that is aerated by peat. Berry growers suggest digging out about 6 or 7 inches of soil and mixing it half-and-half with peat moss. Refill the hole and put in your plants.

Note here that any old peat moss will not do. Look for sphagnum moss because it is more acidic than other types of peat and blueberries do require acid.

A mulch to the depth of several inches is desired. As you know from previous comments I have made about mulch, this achieves several things -- keeps weeds down, keeps moisture up and keeps shallow roots cool.

When harvest time nears, put netting over the bushes, supported by a simple wooden frame or stakes. The birds just love blueberries, too, and are a lot quicker at picking them at their peak than we are.

Blueberry Lemon Bread

My three blueberry bushes provide fresh berries for cereal and desserts but I depend on the grocery store for large quantities. Then I go on a blueberry rampage of jams, preserves and bagging for the freezer. The following tea bread has a very good, refreshing taste. I often take it to meetings when refreshments with tea and coffee are needed. The recipe makes one 8-inch loaf. Don't overdo on the berry quantity, for if you do, it will be too fruity to slice nicely. Use fresh lemon juice instead of bottled for a finer lemon flavor.

Blueberry Lemon Bread

1 ½ cups all-purpose flour
1 teaspoon baking powder
1/4 teaspoon salt
6 tablespoons butter at room temperature
3/4 cup granulated sugar
1/3 cup granulated sugar and 3 tablespoons lemon juice
2 eggs
1 tablespoon grated lemon peel
½ cup milk
1 ½ cups blueberries, fresh or frozen (if frozen, thaw and drain)

Preheat oven to 325 degrees. Grease a 8 ½" x 4 ½" x 2 ½" loaf pan. In a small bowl, combine first 3 ingredients and set aside.
With electric mixer, cream butter and the 3/4 cup sugar until fluffy.
Add eggs, beating well after each one, then add lemon peel.
Mix in dry ingredients alternating with milk.
Gently stir in blueberries.
Spoon batter into pan and bake 1 hour, 15 minutes, or until lightly brown and a toothpick comes out clean.
Meanwhile, combine the 1/3 cup sugar and lemon juice in pan and bring them to a boil, stirring until sugar dissolves. Pierce top of hot loaf several times with a sharp-tined fork and pour the hot lemon mixture over loaf in the pan. Cool for about a half-hour in pan before removing.

What's All this Fuss About Vegetables?

Some people accuse me of being too vegetable-oriented in my gardening. I am, and I'm proud of it, but I grow lots of herbs and flowers as well.

According to the Economic Research Service of the United States Department of Agriculture, the average, at-home food expenditures per person for the year 2000, was $1,633.

That is probably the best rate in most of the world, thanks to American farm production. But in time of recession, fear of job loss, or just wanting to put aside money for other expenses, a vegetable garden can be one place to start lowering that number. Anyway, doesn't a sun-warmed tomato just plucked off the back yard vine taste better than one that was picked from the store's vegetable display?

Thanks to modern home freezers, vegetables can be quickly put aside for winter. When my green beans start producing, I am able to freeze a couple of small sandwich-size bags in the evening after dinner with very little fuss. I might do this several times a week during high production. In little batches, it is no big deal. When winter comes, I'm very glad those bagfuls are there.

Apples, pared and sliced, can be bagged and frozen just as they are for pies and recipes later on. Tomatoes can be frozen fresh with or without the skins and sealed in 1-quart plastic bags. We use our frozen tomatoes in soups or stewed as a dinner vegetable. All this can be done without going to the trouble of getting out the canning jars and canner.

If time permits, my personal preference is to preserve food in glass jars. Then, if there should be a major power failure and loss of freezer use, I would lose very little.

It makes good sense in times of economic instability to "put aside." Why not, and save on something so easy and delicious?

June

Checklist

✔ Use plastic packing "peanuts" in the bottoms of pots for drainage if other things are not immediately available.

✔ Take a tour of your garden every day even though you may not plan on working in it. Insect problems and difficulties that occur can be caught early.

✔ Share the joy. Offer your extra plants after springtime dividing to friends and neighbors.

✔ Reuse laundry scoops for measuring fertilizers. Premark them (1/4 cup, ½ cup, etc.).

✔ Earwigs. They have both good and bad sides. Good -- they eat aphids; bad -- they snack on green plants. Remedy -- sink a tuna can into the soil, leaving some tuna oil or water in it. They will come running, to be captured and disposed of, but decide first whether their benefits outweigh the bad bad effects.

✔ Time to put in peppers, eggplants, melons, beans, coleus and impatiens. They thrive in the warm soil of early June.

✔ Take a few snapshots of your garden from different angles and at different times during the summer. Add these pictures to your journal pages. They will be a guide for future planning.

✔ At our house we opt to continue feeding the birds all summer. We are rewarded by flashes of color from indigo buntings, Baltimore orioles, gold finches and many, many more summer birds.

✔ Tomato plants by now are filling out nicely. If they are not caged yet, do it now before it is necessary to "fight" the branches into confinement.

✔ Japanese beetles are on the fly. Hand pick them and drop into a tin can containing soapy water. We call this work the Beetle Patrol.

✔ Now that spring flowering shrubs are finished blooming, dead head the lilac bushes and spent rhododendron blooms. Trim forsythia back to a manageable shape.

✔ Put in a second planting of green beans so as to lengthen the hearvest season. Put them in where the radishes and lettuces were growing.

✔ FYI Department: It takes a hundred years for Nature to create just one inch of topsoil.

✔ Take a nip or two -- of things like basil, spearmint, chrysanthemums, to produce bushier growth.

✔ Tomatoes produce suckers that grow out of a branch base where it joins the main stem. Nip those, too. You will see it makes the plant bear a little earlier and with larger fruit.

✔ Tie up cauliflower leaves to cover the little white curds that have started to form to keep them white. (See *Cauliflower Culture*, June.)

✔ Mosquito population will be reduced if you make absolutely sure there is no standing water anywhere on your property in which they could breed. (See *Mosquito Control*, June.)

Plan new garden accessories and focal points. We've all seen the "spilled flowerpot" and "garden bed." Recycle an old chair or step ladder and let flowering vines twine over them. Choose morning glory or clematis.

herb of the Month
Comfrey

A family member fell down a set of stairs and got lots of bruises. A friend and herb gardener sent by overnight express a bare-rooted comfrey plant (*Symphytum officinale*). The enclosed note read, "If you don't have comfrey in your own garden for healing purposes, here is one so you'll have it the next time."

That was 3 years ago. I gave it a sunny spot, composted manure and lots of space. I was warned that it can grow 3 to 5 feet tall if not kept pruned.

When it came up the next spring, the vigorous plant was graced with somewhat hairy foliage.

The friend guided me with more information on this healing herb, also colorfully known as knitbone, blackwort and slippery root. She related the benefits of using several of its large, fuzzy leaves as a warm poultice wrapped in warm, moistened cheesecloth and applied to sore muscles and bruises. Dried whole leaves can be used in the winter, moistened in a layer of cheesecloth.

Once established in a garden it will endure forever, it would seem, for another friend said she moved her own plant to a better location and it keeps reappearing every year in the old place no matter how ruthless she is with it.

It blooms with drooping clusters of whitish-blue, yellow or mauve flowers all summer until frost. Keeping the flowers cut off encourages more leaf growth.

If not harvested (cut back) several times each growing season it can become a large bush. With each cutting the leaves can be dried right on the stem and stored in a closed jar or dry place.

I have learned respect for this age-old plant (new to me) and have also made a purchase of cheesecloth just in case we may need it.

> *Lucky for us, because of its hairy leaves, comfrey is one of those plants that is not eaten by deer.*

Wide Rows

In describing use of garden space I have mentioned wide rows and wish to spend a little written space explaining them.

Long ago when it was customary to plant things in single, marching rows, we had a row of carrots, a row of beans. It worked, but since then we have found other gardening methods that work even better. Single rows dry out very fast in the hot summer, making frequent watering a must. That is a wasteful use of precious water. In switching to wide rows I discovered another advantage. Using beans as an example, the plants created their own little microclimate. The moisture from watering lasted longer and their leafy canopy almost eliminated weed growth. Weeds don't like to grow in shady places.

Another advantage of using wide rows is that it gives more than triple the harvest in the same garden space because it removes the need for numerous walking paths, and seeds can be planted closer together. Another advantage is that wide rows will not get compacted from being walked on.

Wide row and raised bed gardening follow the same principles. The difference is that in the latter, the bed is raised and supported by boards or mounding. This is excellent to use where subsoil may be rocky or if it is located in a low, wet area. When planting use a ruler to confirm proper placement of seeds according to the seed packet information.

Harvest is easier, too, because every time you bend or stoop you can reach across almost a whole row. Try it. You will be amazed at the garden yield. Read more about garden bed choices in *The Beauty of Raised Beds*, May, and *To Dig or Not to Dig?* April.

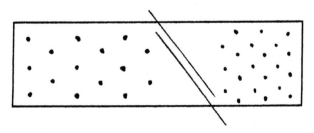

Example of Seed Spacing in Wide Row or Raised Beds.

Strawberry Season
The Basics

When I offer neighbors zucchini, they sort of turn away while saying, "No, thanks." But when I offer strawberries they run to me with open arms. Fresh from the garden, they are everyone's favorite.

For new strawberry growers, there are two kinds of berries from which to choose, so know what you're buying. There are once-a-year bearers and the everbearing. The once-a-year kind produces, obviously, just one crop a year in early summer. Everbearers produce the early summer crop and a second in the fall but are less hardy. The nurseryman can direct you to the one best for your needs.

Make sure the stock you buy is certified to be free of any virus disease.

The location of the strawberry bed should be open and sunny. Soil should have well-rotted manure added to the upper layer of a deeply-dug bed. Also, fork in an all-purpose fertilizer when preparing the bed.

Plan to space the plants about 18 inches apart. If they come in peat pots, soak them about an hour before setting in the soil, pot and all.

Bare rooted ones should be set in quite differently. Dig a hole 1 or 2 inches deeper than the root system, mound the bottom of the hole and spread the roots out over the mound, positioning the upper part of the crown at soil level. Fill in the hole and water. Keep the plants moist during the first several weeks.

If your plants put out blossoms this first season, nip them off. (This will hurt you more than it will hurt them.) Let the roots get firmly established first. They will also put out runners this first year, too. When autumn comes, help conserve the plant's energy by doing a runner-ectomy. These new plants won't need any additional fertilizer now until next year in the late winter.

In the new growing season, tuck clean straw under the plants to keep the berries from touching the ground. Plastic sheeting can be used but make sure the soil is moist before applying. Mark the plants that are doing a terrific job of production. Those are the ones whose new runners will provide more plants for you because a strawberry plant does not bear very heavily after two or three years. Now it's time to get down to business and be tough.

Choose up to 4 of the best runners that come off the stronger plants. Fill 3-inch pots with compost. From each runner pick out the tiny plant that is nearest the parent and sink a filled pot into the soil just beneath it. With a U-shaped bent wire, pin the little plant by the runner to the soil in the pot so it will root there. Pinch off the extra growth beyond the pinned plantlet and now keep the pot watered.

In about 6 weeks new, rooted plants will be ready for moving. By this time, it should be late summer. Sever the runner connecting it to the parent and continue watering. In about a week, transplant to the permanent location and tend exactly as you did the new ones.

Creating New Plants

Of note here is the "layering" type of propagation that is described for strawberries. It can be done also with shrubs such as rhododendron and azaleas. I have done this often. Special plants that you would like to have more of can be easily multiplied.

Start by selecting a branch that is near the bottom of the shrub. Bend it down to touch the ground. Where it touches the ground is where you will prepare it to take root and in a year-and-a-half or two years, it will have established its own root system. Give it another year and it will be ready to sever from the parent plant and moved to its new location.

Where the branch touches the ground, soften the soil by scratching it with a tool and mixing in some compost. Make a few scrapes on the bottom of the branch where it will touch the ground. This is where the new roots will form. Bend the branch down and cover that section with more compost and soil, weighing the covered branch down with a flat rock, brick, pinning it with wire, or in some way making sure that its contact with the soil remains stable. Water for the first few weeks, but after that, nature should take hold for you.

When new shoots and branches are growing from the propagated branch, it is a good sign that it has developed a good root system. Wait for the following year before cutting it from the parent, making sure that its roots are substantial enough to supply its own needs.

A Gardener's Best Friends -- Tools

We are well into the garden season with summer flowers budding and the spring salad vegetables nearly finished, leaving space for the long-awaited summer crops. New garden tools may have been on your shopping list this spring. The old tools that you've had for a long time still work, undoubtedly, but sometimes a new one has been developed that should make gardeners take notice. We all need tools that make our job easier.

I allowed myself the luxury of buying a new hand tool that I experimented with in someone else's garden. Called a Cape Cod weeder, it is a wooden-handled tool that features a 10-inch shank, the last 4 inches of which are turned at a right angle, allowing the angled blade to uproot young weeds. It works well in soft soil, I discovered, and only moderately well in harder soil. However, the angled blade at the end also allows probing to get at the roots of tougher weeds.

Another good one is a plain, 3-pronged claw. It loosens the soil around weeds so they can be easily pulled. The prongs on mine are of a flexible spring-steel and is one of the most comfortable tools I've used.

If you keep a compost pile or need to move mulch around, one of the best tools to invest in would be a five-tined fork, called a mulch fork. Similar to a pitchfork, the curved, narrow, metal tines slide right through the compost or mulch providing lifting power that a shovel wouldn't begin to match.

A gem around the yard and garden is a muck bucket. The one I use came from the housewares department of a large store. Made of sturdy plastic with rope handles, it is a little larger than a bushel basket. It can be pulled around with you as you work, collecting yard waste, which can be added to the compost pile. Saves a lot of steps and is inexpensive. Just pick a color that is compatible with your landscape, for it comes in some neutral colors as well as some very bright ones.

Spend a little time looking around the stores for new ideas. It may pay off and ease your garden work.

Let's Discuss This
Weed Problem

By the time the weather turns hot in mid- or late June, weeds have managed to get a strangle-hold in everyone's garden. Unless one is vigilant early in the season, these weeds by now have become very tough, and almost defiant, their roots seemingly reaching downward farther than they can be pulled up.

A relatively weed-free garden is a pleasure to look at and to work in. But more than that, it means that tender annuals and perennials won't be in competition with an army of weeds for moisture and nutrients, for weeds are very greedy and hungry.

When time began, they evolved for the purpose of covering the bare planet. They do a good job of it. And in evolving, they learned to be enduring and tough. Each weed plant produces tens of thousands of seeds in a very short time. The seeds act as time-release capsules do -- they don't all sprout at once. Many can lie dormant for weeks, months or years before conditions are right to trigger germination.

Many weeds do not depend on their seeds alone, but on underground runners. They can be hoed away or pulled out, but any scraps of root that remain in the ground often re-sprout into vigorous plants. Mulch can be the one solution for our gardens that makes the most sense. Mulch has been discussed in other sections of this book. It is a very valuable tool for gardeners. (See *Removing the Mystery of Mulch*, April.)

Our tender annuals, perennials and all our hybrids have not inhabited nor evolved on the earth for as long as weeds. My advice to help beat the weeds is to take a tour of your garden every day or two. Just spending 15 minutes at a time to remove the small ones can be a valuable benefit. When the same weed has had its top pulled off enough times, its resistance declines, it becomes weakened by being repeatedly defoliated, and you're beginning to win the battle.

So the bottom line is to weed often; weed regularly, and get the mulch laid down.

Insect Insights
Lightning Bugs, a.k.a. Fireflies

An invitation at ten o'clock one evening took us to a neighbor's house to sit in the field by his barn to watch the "light show." I thought he meant we would watch comets or fireworks.

The light show was fireworks, indeed, but in the form of masses of sparkling fireflies doing what they do best in the evening hours of summer -- lighting up the world using their unique method of communicating with flashes and blinks, reminding us of many little Tinkerbells. This enchanting light show can only be seen in the eastern half of the United States where these insects live.

In the neighbor's barnyard where a moon had not yet risen, we noticed different firefly displays from different species. Some emitted long blinks of undulating intensities, some used staccato-type blinks. Some blinked 3 or 4 times in a row, some signaled for 10 or 12.

We observed a single firefly blinking dimly from a spot on the side of the barn. Examination with a penlight, revealed it was enjoying an evening meal of spider a la carte.

Fireflies are soft-bodied insects with hard black/brown wing covers. During the day they rest and eat in the grass where it is moist. In the evening they fly up to meet their mates. Males do all the flashing, an activity that we could call "sparking."

They lay their eggs in the grass and hatch in about 4 weeks. When they hatch, the larvae actually glow, hence the name glow worms. By summer's end, they have become much larger from weeks of feeding and can be seen in the grass at night sending out an eerie glimmer. In the autumn take a walk around your yard after dark and you'll see them. These glow worms will hibernate during the winter and mature in the spring to become the delightful fireflies that light up our lives.

The best part of this whole story is that they are beneficial insects, consuming snails, slugs, cutworms and many insect pest larvae.

Over the years, use of chemicals for insect control and the suburban desire for closely-cut lawns have dramatically decreased firefly population. However, you can still court them back to your environment by limiting chemical use and by allowing wildflowers and tall grasses to grow in garden areas. Then on an evening in June sit back and count how many variations of firefly messages you can see.

Tasty Geraniums

Geraniums are those stalwarts of sunny, summer gardens, drought tolerant and blooming in all shades of red, pink and white. They come in more than 200 scents and flavors, so are a natural for flavorings in cold, summer beverages.

Any flavor geranium can be used but lemon and rose are the most traditional ones. Snip a few leaves off your plant, wash and pat dry. Cut off the stems. Find a jar with a screw-top lid and layer about a half-inch of sugar in the bottom. Lay one leaf on top of the sugar and add another half-inch of sugar. Continue layering sugar and leaves until the jar is filled. Seal the jar tightly and store in a cool, dark place for several weeks. The sugar will become permeated with the wonderful scent of your geranium leaves and give a different innovation to your cold drinks.

Lavender Lemonade

In comparing recipes for lavender lemonade with a friend we came up with a tempting drink for hot weather.

Thaw a can of frozen pink lemonade mix. Meanwhile, pick enough leaves of lavender to fill a half-cup, chopped. Blossoms can be used instead of leaves, measuring a half-cup of blossoms. Drop the chopped leaves or blossoms into a quart of boiling water. Let steep for 3 minutes. Strain and cool. Use this water when diluting the thawed pink lemonade mix, adding more water as the can directions suggest. Pour over ice cubes and garnish with a fresh stem or two of lavender blossoms or a sprig of leaves.

Your guests will keep coming back for more.

Pretty Perennials – Why and how?

Perennials are those plants that are as permanent a fixture in your garden as you can find. They come up faithfully every spring, bloom brightly on schedule and seem to take care of themselves. They die down at the end of the season or with the first frosts, only to remain dormant until springtime. One need buy perennials only once, compared to annuals which must be replaced each year.

When buying, check the tags for bloom color, mature height and spread, light and water requirements. Tall plants would be placed toward the center in a free-standing bed, or in the back of a border; shorter ones concentrated toward the front. In creating or redesigning a bed make a scale drawing on paper. If this doesn't help in planning, make a grid across the beds with string in one-foot squares. Locate tall ones such as delphinium, nicotiana, phlox, monarda, liatris in the back of a border type bed or in the center of a free-standing one. Any plants that would be placed in front of them should be of shorter stature, such as clusters of sweet William, sedum, dwarf marigold. In front of them, use things like alyssum, ageratum, portulaca.

Color enters the picture now. Color combinations are for your choosing, such as all pinks with reds and whites; blues, purples and whites, or a scheme to give a golden glow with Stella d'Oro lilies, rudbeckia (black-eyed Susans), red-centered shasta daisies, sparked with clusters of white daisies and dianthus.

If you do not wish to follow a color scheme at all, then there is nothing wrong with a wide variety of colors. After all, the wildly-assorted colors of British cottage gardens are just as attractive.

In caring for perennials, removing faded blossoms keeps new ones coming and eliminates unsightly vegetation. Stake taller varieties even if they do not show signs of leaning. A heavy rainstorm can quickly force them down. Use mulch, of course, to keep roots cool, moist and to reduce weed sprouts.

One can almost never go wrong with perennials. In the fall their spent stalks should be removed to eliminate a haven for over-wintering insects. The plants will come back in the spring with renewed vigor. (See *Dependable Perennials*, July, for suggestions.)

The Subject is Roses
Choosing the Best for Your Needs

June is the month of roses. Much has been written of them in song and sonnet since ancient times. Their fragrance is so overwhelmingly sweet, how can we live without them?

I used to think there were 2 kinds -- climbers and bushes. I also thought the color choices were red, white, pink and yellow. How naive. When I decided to grow some of my own a new world opened up.

It takes a sunny place for roses -- 6 or more hours of daily sun. Only a very few varieties will tolerate a little shade.

When shopping for roses, choices are not simple to make. It is important to know growth and blooming habits, and nuances of color. Rose growers are very careful in their catalogues to provide the most accurate shades of color on the printed page. To get a very good idea of what are available, look at the Jackson & Perkins and Arena Rose Company catalogs, the addresses of which are in the January section of this book. You will enjoy hundreds of color photographs.

Have an idea of what space is available in your yard and how many hours of sunlight that space receives. The buyer should also know how the rose will be used in the garden; for instance, will it accent an existing flower bed, provide fragrance at an entry way or porch, to cut off an unpleasant view, to dramatize a length of fence, or simply to use for cutting. Your last consideration might be color choice.

Roses fall into categories, or classes, so you must be familiar with some terms before shopping to avoid confusion.

Climbing roses are large-blossomed and usually everblooming. Older varieties had only one or two blooming periods and have been replaced with newer everbloomings. Blossoms are clustered on the stems such as floribunda would be. Popular climbers are the familiar Blaze (red) or New Dawn (pink). They do not actually climb, as a vine would, but produce long canes which must be supported by trellis or lattice, or an arbor. Their canes are tied up so they don't sprawl.

Florabunda type has many blooms per stem, produced in clusters but smaller in size than the climber.

Grandifloras are tall, stately bushes, vigorous in growth habits. They produce individual blooms, several to a stem. The pink Queen Elizabeth is a favorite of this class.

Hybrid Tea is the most popular of rose bushes that produces the long-stemmed rose. Here, the color range is enormous -- many offering variegated or several-toned shades. Chrysler Imperial (red) and John F. Kennedy (white) are prime examples of the hybrid tea.

Tree roses are less popular but are the most elegant of all. Many can be container-grown for deck, patio or doorway accents.

Shrub rose is still another type which is used for multiple plantings such as for hedging. Not readily available in garden stores, they can be ordered through catalogs. They are shrub-like in growth, reaching proportions of 4 to 5 feet tall and 4 feet in width. Their everblooming quality makes the perfect summer vista as field borders, available in standard colors.

(A note here should make the reader aware that decades ago the May-flowering, single, white multiflora rose was sold everywhere, even by the U.S. Government, as a viable solution for creating hedgerows of lasting quality. Multiflora is a shrub rose now considered aggressively invasive. It is a scourge of the farming industry. Be a responsible gardener. If it is offered for sale anywhere, steer clear of this particular rose variety.)

Check your garden layout. Considering how many beautiful varieties of rose bushes there are, there must be room someplace in your garden for a few.

Of Weeds and Wildflowers
Daisy

She loves me; she loves me not. The common white daisy (*Chrysanthemum leucanthemum*) has a maligned past but is much loved by nearly everyone. It is known by many names, among them, ox-eye daisy, marguerite, button daisy and field daisy.

When this nation still belonged to the American Indians, the eastern half of it was totally forested. Settlers came and transformed it from forestland to farmland. That is when the daisy appeared, brought quite accidentally, in grain products from Europe, in ballast on ships and in mud on boots and tools.

> "The common daisy has a maligned past, but is much-loved by nearly everyone."

This daisy does not grow in shady forestland but flourishes in full sun, and usually is happier in poorer soil than richer soil. The plant is tough and durable and produces lots of seeds. It took over the eastern part of this continent in sunny spots along roadsides and farm field edges and wherever else land was temporarily empty. It filled the earth with waves of snowy white and soon became the bane of every farmer. Special efforts to uproot the plants took hard work and lots of time, for no chemical herbicides were even dreamed of then.

As time passed and farmland has become paved highways, subdivisions and parking lots, the daisy has nearly disappeared from the landscape. Now we see it tended in gardens, a reminder of days not long ago when fields of daisies thrived and lovers counted petals of it and made wreaths for a damsel's head.

Oh, Deer

Gardeners have been plagued by overpopulation of the eastern white tail deer for many years and the problem does not go away; it increases. Two schools of thought prevail. One is that the deer population should be reduced by any means. The other is that deer are peaceful creatures who were here before we started growing things that they love to eat. Wherever you stand on the issue, it still requires knowlege of methods to thwart browsing deer from your yard.

Fawns are born in the spring. They rarely move more than a mile from where they were born. Deer are diurnal and browse in the evening and early morning, stripping shrubs of leaves and buds. They can make hostas disappear overnight. Daylilies get chomped off. Yew is a popular target, as well as English holly and tulips. (A more complete list appears in Appendix.) We hear of things that deer "won't" eat but all plants are vulnerable when there is a large herd or a severe winter, making food scarce. If your garden happens to be on one of their habitual paths, there is not much hope, short of 10-foot fencing or large dogs.

There are commercial remedies to repel deer , but many gardeners, in frustration, have devised other means of deflecting deer interest.

A friend has acres of well-tended, prize shrubs. He found that deer are smart and have paths through his woods and fields to good browsing places. These paths are taught to fawns so the youngsters soon learn where the best-tasting plants are along those paths. He has caged many of his most valuable shrubs with chicken wire. Fishing line is another trick, threading a 60-lb test line back and forth many times creating an invisible barrier that redirects deer's attention. He also uses a radio outside connected to a timer that turns on and off sporatically. The stations of choice are a news station or talk show. Other gardeners tie small, nylon-stocking bags with pieces of heavily-perfumed soap, or clumps of barber shop hair on branches they hope to protect. Still others spread blood meal around, or a solution of egg and water painted on leaves which must be renewed after each rain. Lengths of chicken wire can be laid flat on the ground which deer will not walk over.

We wage our battles and change tactics often, but must be resigned to the fact that Bambi is here to stay.

Mosquito Control

West Nile Virus, carried by infected mosquitos, can cause West Nile encephalitis and is commonly found in humans, birds and other animals in Africa, Eastern Europe, the Far and Middle East. Until 1999, it had never been documented in the Western Hemisphere. An outbreak of it occurred that year in New York City, probably introduced into this country by an infected bird or mosquito.

Although the disease has not yet spread to our region, the following advice is offered by the Environmental Protection Agency which every home owner should heed to help reduce mosquito breeding grounds. Their suggestions will help protect everyone from contact with mosquitos.

♦ Change water weekly or more often in birdbaths, wading pools, flower pot trays or any other receptacle that holds water.

♦ Any empty buckets, flower pots, containers of any kind should be turned over so there is no opportunity for even an inch of collected water to stand.

♦ Keep rain gutters cleaned out so there is no standing water in them.

♦ Keep swimming pools treated and circulating.

♦ When outside, use mosquito repellants, smoke coils and citronella, following directions carefully.

♦ Check window and door screens for proper fitting, keeping them closed tightly.

♦ Wear long pants and long sleeves and head netting when working outside and in areas where mosquitos are known to breed.

There will be a higher mosquito population during a damp summer than a dry one. They do not breed in water that is moving, as in a flowing creek, pond with a fountain or waterfall. In rain barrels, add a goldfish or two which will eat larvae that may develop. Lay screening across the top of a rain barrel to prevent mosquitos from entering, or use floating disks of Bt. They can be bought at garden stores.

Additional information is available from Penn State's West Nile Web Site: www.pested.psu.edu/spWestNile and from Pennsylvania Department of Health Web Site: www.westnile.state.pa.us/, or call 1-887-724-3258.

Leaping Lizards

Why don't you invite some toads and frogs to live in your garden? Then you can retire that electronic bug zapper. These little four-footed insectivores are known to eat 3 times their weight in insects every day. That's the best deal you can get.

Toads and frogs are called amphibians which means they spend part of their lives in water or moist surroundings and the other part of their lives on land. They can be either "tailed" (salamanders) or "untailed" (toads and frogs). They lay jelly-covered eggs in water which develop into tadpoles. These tadpoles feed on microscopic junk in the water until they develop legs. As they mature, they become air-breathing adults, leave their wet place, and go back to water again only to mate and lay eggs next spring. Meanwhile, they zap slugs, flies, cutworms, beetles, sowbugs and ants. But we are not done with their menus yet -- they also love grasshoppers, gypsy moths and centipedes. Salamanders eat their share of insects as well and are welcome visitors to any garden.

This little pest control service can be coaxed to take up residence in your yard. Requirements are not difficult for the landlord to provide. Make a place for them by letting a section of your yard become a little wild. It isn't as bad as it sounds. This little "wild" place can consist of rocks, ferns and bushy shrubs under which your small boarders will find a place to hide. They will burrow beneath mulch, old straw or grass clippings. If you want to, provide additional cool shade by installing a "toad abode" in their wild area. It can be a store-bought red clay frog hut or an overturned, broken flower pot, but it should be kept out of the sun. Moisten the area with a hose during dry spells to keep them happy.

If you already have a breeding ground for them in the way of a small pond, make it a fishless pond. Fish eat amphibian eggs and tadpoles. Toads and frogs will avoid ponds that use pumps or waterfalls. Sink pans or birdbath tops into mulch or soil in the shady wild corner and place a few stones in the water for hopping in or out. This little reservoir, changed often, will provide them with drinking water. It is interesting to watch the frog hotel for newcomers, leaving them undisturbed of course, as they help take control of the bug population in their new neighborhood.

Decorating Flower Beds with Vegetables

The custom of growing vegetables in a spot segregated from other plants has been around for ages. Thousands of years ago Romans and Greeks grew ornate, ornamental gardens for show and banished the edibles to another place out of sight. In the Middle Ages, life became extremely unsteady so food gardens became vital and often included herbs for medicinal use and culinary flavorings. As North America became colonized, the first priority of settlers was to carve places from the forest for gardens that would grow food and herbs, and were, incidentally, fenced to protect against wild critters. As life became easier, flowers were added for their beauty and grass lawns were developed on properties of the affluent. So the food garden became secondary and usually was kept out of sight. Times change, thankfully, and now we can enjoy all manner of home-grown plants in a single bed.

> *"...new varieties of vegetables have been bred that allow them to compete for attention in any flower bed."*

In recent years new varieties of vegetables have been bred that allow them to compete for attention in any flower bed. Bright Lights Swiss Chard, is one (see *Chalk it Up to Chard*, March). Some pepper cultivars are a wonderful example to include in the flower bed. For example, Prairie Fire pepper sports tiny red, orange and yellow peppers all at one time The multi-colored bell peppers come in shades of not only green, red, orange and yellow, but also purple. You will find some pepper varieties with purple and also variegated foliage. Lettuces vary from light yellow-green to deep red. Basils are a natural in flower beds and can be included in bouquets for the house. The list of colorful and different types of vegetables goes on and on. There is flowering kale, Savoy cabbage, okra, sages such as pineapple or tri-color, yellow pear or yellow cherry tomatoes and eggplants producing small, white, egg-shaped fruits.

Again, review seed catalogs for the culture of any of these above-mentioned and for additional ideas to create your own style.

Checklist

✔ July sometimes is a down time for gardens because most of the hard work is already done. Now is the time to spend tending, waiting for and enjoying the harvests. Don't let up on the daily inspection tours to spot what's going on among your green friends.

✔ No matter how tiring outside work is, take the effort to put away garden tools when work is done. Repeated exposure to sun and rain eventually rots wooden handles, making them splintery and weak. It also allows the rusting process to start on metal parts.

✔ Peas and beans that have gone beyond their prime on the bush can be dried, shelled and stored in a jar for winter cooking. Make sure they are being given enough drying time before storing to prevent hidden moisture that would encourage mold growth.

✔ After July 4th, pull out all the pea vines, sprinkle the soil lightly with 5-10-5 or 10-10-10 fertilizer, water in, wait several days, then plant fall crops such as lettuce, broccoli, cabbages, carrots. Until they get established, keep the soil moist and shaded when dry spells occur.

✔ Last two weeks of July is usually peak production time for green beans and zucchinis. If your vacation falls at that time, ask someone to come in and pick every-other day. They may keep the vegetables and your plant production will not falter.

✔ Dispose of used coffee grounds in the compost pile, or they may be spread on the soil outside. They are helpful in repelling cutworms and other soft-bodied insects, as well as adding an organic component to the soil.

✔ Deadhead spent flowers. Instead of seed production, you would rather have more flower production. Do this every several days to petunias, pansies, geraniums and other summer bloomers. Cut back spent feverfew blossoms, as well, for a second blooming in late summer. It is easier to work with a pair of scissors than fingernails.

✔ Blueberry plants should be kept watered, especially during dry spells. Their roots are shallow and they don't react well to "hot feet".

✔ Keep cucumbers moist and cool by watering often and applying mulch. Cucumbers and melons require more water than most other vegetables.

✔ Mint produces enormous quantities of leaves. For drying, pick in the morning after the dew has dried. Add fresh, chopped, mint leaves to steamed, buttered carrots. Also serve a dish of peas with mint sprigs as garnish. Add sprigs or stems to any glass of iced tea or lemonade. When making sun tea, add a handful of mint to the jar along with the tea bags.

✔ Your fresh garden dill is a wonderful addition to pot pie or meat pie pastry. Just add a generous tablespoonful or two to your pastry.

✔ When watering plants which have received a lot of TLC, be aware there are right ways and wrong ways. See *Have a Drink*, July.

✔ A cure for some insect pests is to keep something like a birdbath top in the bed filled with water to invite predator wasps, birds and mantids to drink and bathe there. You will want them to notice the edible bugs nearby and eat them. Change the water every several days.

✔This may be the perfect time of year to step back and take note whether your garden looks messy, weedy and generally out of control. If so, perhaps downsizing next year should be in order. Feeling overwhelmed by garden chores is a clue that a change in gardening responsibilities should be made.

✔ A frustrating abundance of diseases and pests could indicate that there is too little air circulation. If you've experienced this, try relocating the garden to a better spot or plant less closely.

> *Before leaving on vacation, water deeply as many of your plants as possible.*

have a Drink

Summer time can become hot and dry. It's what we fondly refer to as, "the good old summertime." Heat usually isn't the worst of it; it can be the dryness from a temporary or extended drought. Those of us who use well water are careful how much water goes into the garden that we need for the house. And when we do water the gardens, we should know the must efficient ways to do it.

We learn to collect water from the kitchen and store it until needed. Water that would be collected for plants would include that which fruit and vegetables are rinsed in, hand-washing water, and the first water that is run from the hot water tap before it becomes hot.

Dish pan water has some limitations for use. It is all right to use in the garden, but not if the detergent contains boron or bleach. Otherwise, don't use it more than once or twice a week. It should also not be used on vegetables or on acid-loving plants such as rhododendrons, ferns, azaleas, but it can be applied to all other types of plants.

If you would like to test how deeply your garden is watered, use a sturdy stick or a one-half-inch rod. Push it into the soil. Where the soil is damp, it should slide easily, but where soil is dry, it will stop. Watering is adequate when moisture seeps to a depth of 4 to 6 inches.

Gardens, in general, need about one inch of rain per week. When some flowers, in particular shade plants, wilt on a hot afternoon, hold off with the water and check those same plants the next morning. If they still look droopy, give them a drink. Otherwise, they are usually all right as they are.

Watering too often, such as on a daily basis or when not needed encourages roots to develop too near the surface. Let up on the frequent waterings in order to allow roots to reach deeper into the soil where moisture lies.

Don't forget that mulch is an aid. It helps to drought-proof by holding moisture in the soil. Add it to a depth of about 2 or 3 inches on top of soil that is already moist. Plants that have been protected by a 3-inch layer of mulch will be kept as much as 15 degrees cooler than beds left unprotected.

There are many ways to water gardens when conservation is necessary. It doesn't have to be burdensome. Just select the method or methods that suit your situation. If those don't work well for you, try others.

❧ When planting, build a small berm around each plant to create a saucer-sized depression at the stems. This causes rain water to seep in and not run off.

❧ Let the garden hose drip or trickle at the rootball of shrubs or specific plants. It can be moved in a half-hour to a different location.

❧ Buy a length of soaker hose and lay it along a bed or a row. It will trickle or "sweat" moisture into the soil.

❧ Timers can be bought and attached near the faucet at the house, set to turn water on or off at certain times.

❧ Save empty coffee cans and punch holes into the bottoms. Sink them into the ground beside plants and keep them filled. If water runs out too fast or doesn't run out at all, adjust the holes.

❧ Establish a rain barrel to collect water. It will stay in place permanently and can be under a shortened downspout. Even if your rain barrel were to be set in place now, at least the occasional summer thunderstorm would be a source of water. To keep it from stagnating and attracting mosquitos, put in a couple of inexpensive goldfish. An alternative to wooden rain barrels (which must contain water in order to become water-tight) is a trash can or other large receptacle.

❧ One of the benefits of watering from a rain barrel is that the water has had time to warm a bit. Water coming straight from the hose is often very cold which can stun plants into momentarily stopping their growth.

❧ Modern science can help as well. Polymers (the stuff that retains moisture in diapers) are available in granular form from garden stores. Only a spoonful applied to the soil at the time of planting helps keep moisture in for a longer period of time. Use only the recommended amount even though it might not seem like enough.

❧ If watering with a sprinkler, the best time is in the morning to allow wet leaves to dry as the morning advances. Evening watering can promote fungus growth when leaves remain wet overnight. This kind of overhead watering is very wasteful with much of the water running into gullies and evaporating into the air. It should be very low on the list of choices.

Have fun combating dry spells and reach for the challenge.

Take Time to
Stop and Eat the Flowers

An interesting aspect of summer picnics and company meals is the use of flowers as food garnishes. The practice of floral garnishes and flavorings is an old one that once fell by the wayside, but has been delightfully revived.

Blossoms of chives and onions can top any salad, as can the fanciful, spiky flowers of bee balm (*Monarda*). Add red sage (*Salvia*) as a garnish to cucumber salads by breaking up the blossoms and sprinkling over the cucumbers. Lemon Gem dwarf marigold is one that adds a citrus flavor to a fish or tuna salad plate. The blue flowers of rosemary and lavender blossoms of eggplant are also a nice, edible addition.

Stems of lavender (mentioned in *Lavender Lemonade*, June), can also be used to "spike" the sugar bowl. Add a new dimension to apple jelly by placing a stem or two of lavender into the jar before pouring the home-made jelly into it.

Geranium leaves can flavor sugar for beverages. (see *Tasty Geraniums*, June.) One geranium leaf added to the bottom of a jelly jar when pouring in hot apple jelly can pleasantly alter the taste.

Nasturtium has an ancient culinary history. Seed pods were once steeped in vinegar as a substitute for capers. A blossom and a leaf or two make a sandwich or salad garnish with a pleasing peppery flavor.

Violet blossoms and leaves are favored as an enhancement to desserts. As well, calendula petals can be added as a garnish for fruit salads.

Besides blossoms, the foliage of many plants offers a wide variety of color and texture. Flowering kale, sage in colors of grey and purple, basil of purple, mahogany and green, red cabbage leaves, beet tops, the ferny leaves of carrots, asparagus and dill are all good examples.

Squash blossom buds are palatable dipped in batter and lightly fried. Wild daylily flowers can be steamed until they are just wilted, then seasoned with butter and salt. I am told by a friend that the green buds of the wild daylily make nice outdoor snacking. They can also be cut crosswise as a topping for salads.

Keep in mind that any plant part that has come in contact with insecticides or any chemical must not be used for eating.

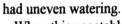 Eggplant Strategies

S omeone complained to me about the eggplants he grew. He puts in only two or three plants every year but he would like them to taste *good*. The complaint was about bitterness. What can be more disappointing than expecting a home-grown vegetable to taste perfect and it greets the palate with bitterness?

Another gardener suggested a reason by saying, "He let them stay on the plant too long." But another underlying reason for bitterness in taste could be a stressed plant...one that has not had adequate water or has had uneven watering.

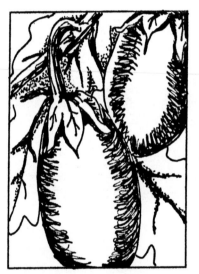

When this vegetable is mature, no matter what its size, it will be glossy and smooth. Over mature fruit will be dullish in appearance and even slightly faded in color. This may happen while you are away on vacation and are not monitoring on a daily basis.

When your eggplants are ready for harvest, they do not break or twist off readily. Be prepared with a pair of pruners or knife.

In windy weather or dry July and August, they need an inch of water per week. So do peppers, tomatoes and squash.

Another tip on eggplant growing is the use of Epsom salts. A neighbor uses it all the time on tomatoes and I've seen it work. The salts provide magnesium, making faster-maturing fruit. It works on peppers as well.

Try this formula: 2 tablespoons of Epsom salts in one gallon of water. Apply to the soil as blossoms begin to bloom.

After harvesting, eggplants are ready to serve immediately or can be refrigerated for up to three days.

This vegetable is sometimes attacked by flea beetles. Read *Insect Insights* for August.

Insect Insights
Wasps and Yellow Jackets

Everyone recoils and does the "get-away-from-me" dance when wasps or yellow jackets appear at a picnic. It is little-known that both these insects are beneficial and deserving of a second thought. Yes, they land on your watermelon and hang around beverage containers, but see them from another point of view, if you can.

The yellow jacket is considered a wasp. The queen builds a small paper nest somewhere in house eves or in an old mouse burrow in the ground. The wasp's first brood become the workers to forage and feed the queen and her succeeding broods. Winter kills all but the queen, when she seeks refuge under a piece of tree bark or some other sheltered spot until spring comes.

"Wasps and yellow jackets are important pollinators, along with honeybees, but are also important pest predators."

Wasps and yellow jackets are important pollinators, along with honey bees, but are also important pest predators. They dive into foliage and come away with flies, caterpillars and larvae to feed their young. Unlike honey bees which feed their young on pollen, wasps and yellow jackets raise their families on "bugburgers." They help control whiteflies and aphids. Some wasps live on hornworms, laying eggs beneath the skin. They draw nutrition and moisture from the hornworm, causing it to die.

Believe it or not, wasps actually are not hostile by nature and will not sting unless they are being provoked. While they feed on caterpillars and other insects, they also feed on nectar, juices from fruit and our picnic foods. Avoid contact with them at picnics by keeping food and drinks covered. Citronella candles may help repel them where people congregate, but in dry weather, they become thirsty and cranky. Keep several birdbaths available with fresh water.

It is probably best that the gray paper nests of these insects be destroyed if they are where people gather or if someone in your family is allergic to stings. Otherwise, consider them friendly.

118

Leaf Miners

By now, if you have an infestation of leaf miners, you'll know it from the little tan tunnels and trails you will see woven through the leaves of certain plants. These markings seem to be inside the leaves themselves, between the top and bottom layers of each leaf. Plants affected most often are chard, spinach, nasturtiums, bean plants, columbine and sweet peas. But other plants are affected as well. Be on the lookout for these markings inside leaves and know what to do about them.

> *"Plants should never be crowded. When they are, air circulation can be hampered and insects will find it a good place to set up house-keeping."*

The critters making the trail patterns are the larvae of the adult leaf miner which is a small fly. The tiny black dots inside the trails are the excrement of the larvae.

There are several controls to use.

Plants should never be crowded, for if they are, air circulation can be hampered and insects will find it a good place to set up housekeeping.

Remove all weeds and debris in and around the garden. These are favorite places for most insects to take refuge.

When any miner damage is noticed, pick off the affected leaves and destroy. Inspect the undersides of other leaves to locate eggs. Scratch them off with a fingernail.

Companion plants, such as marigolds and garlic can also be used to repel them.

Another control is Bacillus Thuringienses, also called BT. It can be bought in all garden centers. This is a biological disease that will kill the leaf miners in their larval stage but is not toxic to birds, pets or humans.

Pretty as a Petunia

Plant some pretty petunias for a full season of colorful blooms. These cheerful, ruffly flowers come in a wide variety of colors that can be used everywhere in your garden -- to trail in hanging baskets, to overflow in well-placed containers, along pathways, driveways, on porches and decks. They absolutely flourish in full sun. They are not a good choice for cool, shady nooks. Full sun means 6 or more hours of direct sun per day. Their requirements for best performance are right up there with things like tomatoes and marigolds. If placed in a spot that receives shade for part of the day, branches will become leggy and will produce fewer flowers, but can still add color to your scheme. When using window boxes, remember that overhanging eaves may interfere with the amount of rain water they would receive, so plan to provide that yourself.

Petunias are not particular about their soil requirements. They are very adaptable and will grow in almost any kind -- even in sandy or clay composition -- but, of course, will do best in a light, rich soil that has good drainage. A layer of mulch may need to be added to cover the soil, especially around the double-flowered varieties, to keep mud splashes off the flowers.

The best time for planting is on a cloudy or overcast day. Set them into the soil at the same level that they were growing in the market pack.

They do not require a lot of care, but do not want to be ignored, either. Fertilize monthly with a general fertilizer. They are drought-tolerant and do not need to be kept wet or moist. You will find they are excellent flowers for cutting and will even grow better if pruned and deadheaded on a frequent basis.

Choose colors that will make an attractive focal point in your landscape.

Petunias are great in hanging baskets.
Combine them with grey-leaved, trailing
helichrysum (licorice) or artemisia.

Containing Your Garden

When garden spaces are too small for all your plans, or there happens to be a colorless corner somewhere in your yard, container gardening may be the answer. Any container will do as either a temporary or permanent one, but be prepared to take it into the house for the winter. Freezing weather can cause pots to crack. An option to leaving pots outside in freezing weather can be to elevate them on bricks or pot feet so complete drainage can take place.

One needn't depend solely on clay or plastic planters. If an object holds soil it's viable. An old tea kettle, length of clay pipe, a rusty bucket all stretch the imagination and add whimsical effects. Use a wicker basket loaded with impatiens and ivy. Groupings of containers of various sizes can be rearranged when the need arises.

Remember that in using planters of any kind, moisture will evaporate quickly in the heat of full sun. They will need watering often -- sometimes more than once a day. Clay dries out faster than plastic or wood, but clay and wood help keep soil and roots cooler than plastics. A steady breeze, even if cool, can be very drying.

Fertilize container plants more often than those growing directly in the

ground, for their roots are limited to only what's in the pot. Do not be discouraged if it seems that they take extra care. You will love them and won't mind the trouble because they are fulfilling a need. When planting more than one variety in a container, use plants that have the same requirements such as all shade or all sun tolerant. In an appealing grouping, they would be of different heights and colors. For instance, an asparagus fern offers texture and height, coleus offers height as well as color; a trailing vinca softens.

Drainage holes in the bottom are necessary, but if it is not practical to add them, put about 2 inches of pebbles in the bottom. Moisten the potting soil thoroughly, then plant and wait for the show to begin.

herb of the Month
Feverfew

Feverfew is one of my favorite summer herbs because no matter how I neglect it, it keeps coming back. I am learning to be kinder and gentler toward this nice, white-flowered, summer plant because now I understand what an important fixture it is in my own yard.

Feverfew is a pest-free perennial, and can be ranked among the Dependable Perennials as described in the next article. It reseeds itself rather freely and is so eager to please, it even comes up in the grass. Feverfew (*Chrysanthemum parthenium*) is a very old-fashioned plant, smelling very much like its name implies -- chrysanthemum -- and was one that probably grew in grandmother's garden. It certainly was a stand-by in my mother's.

I use its cut flowers for arrangements and find they are long-lasting. The only thing it really demands is to be cut back after initial blooming to allow new growth and another crop of flowers to develop.

> *"Feverfew is known to be a fairly good insect repellant and good to rub on insect bites."*

It grows best in full sun to partial shade, and in my yard where it takes over, it receives that partial shade. It is on the north side of the house. Not much else grows there, so I appreciate its company. The soil there is light and well-drained, making it suitable for feverfew.

Over its long history it has been used extensively for a wide assortment of ills, from arthritis and infant colic to toothache. Feverfew is known to be a fairly good insect repellant and good to rub on insect bites.

If including feverfew in your flower garden, you not likely to be disappointed in its performance.

Dependable Perennials

There are certain plants that persist in gardens everywhere because they are nearly indestructible. They perform admirably year after year and do not put much demand on our attention. Many perennials act like prima donnas that need careful division before they strangle themselves or they may get frosted because they couldn't stand some severe weather. If you are looking for the first kind -- the dependable ones -- here are some suggestions.

Columbines (*Aquilegia vulgaris,* full sun/part shade) reseed themselves generously. They hybridize themselves and one never knows what colors will be produced by seed the next time around. Each year treat yourself to a few new ones of a different color, for eventually, if let to go over the years, your columbines will all become a soft lavender. That color is not unpleasing, but the introduction of new colors keep the interest going.

Lamb's Ears (*Stachys Byzantina,* full sun) can be used along patio edges, walks and steps. Its soft grey foliage contrasts with the bright colors of other plants nearby. The magenta blossoms, however, draw bees from miles around. If that is a danger, the flower stalks may be cut off. Plants can become flattened somewhat in very humid, hot weather, but will perk up as soon as the weather becomes favorable. Lamb's ears are long-lived and extremely hardy.

Peonies (*Paeonia,* full sun) live virtually forever. Unfortunately, peony flowers can get overloaded and fall down in a heavy rain so they should be staked. If their site is somewhat shady they will still bloom, but on weak stems. Staking is a must for those. They do not transplant well and often take years to bloom again. It will be less disappointing to buy a new one instead.

Tiger lily (*Lilium tigrinum,* full sun/partial shade) is a striking orange and black lily. This tall plant keeps coming back and coming back, spreading by way of little black bulblets that drop to the ground and take hold to bloom in another two years. Tiger lilies do not have particular soil or care requirements, being quite independent bloomers in July and August.

Purple coneflowers (*Echinacea purpurea*, full sun) are prairie flowers but now are also perennials in many gardens. They are tough plants which bloom from June to September, in shades of rosy-purple with a soft brown center. The flowers attract butterflies and in the winter, goldfinches come to eat the seeds. Although coneflowers require full sun, they will tolerate some shade.

Black-eyed susans (*Rudbeckia*, also called coneflower, full sun). They are sister plants to the purple coneflower, being a prairie flower, too. Now in perennial gardens they offer masses of golden blooms through most of the summer. They are very hardy and insect-free.

Coral bells (*Heuchera*, full sun/partial shade) are a reliable addition to any garden. Their leaves have a mounding habit of growth, from which come tall stems of flowers in June. The old standard variety has flame-pink flowers above a green mound. Newer varieties are even more appealing, such as the Purple Palace or Midnight Claret, with striking mahogany-purple-metalic leaves that seem to change colors in the sun, with stems of small white flowers. Many gardeners appreciate deep colors of the leaves and use them as accents among lighter-colored foliage, cutting off the incidental flower stalks. However you like to display them is up to you, but it's a winner of a garden plant.

Amsonia (*Amsonia hubrectii*, full sun/partial shade). Also known as blue star because of its clusters of starry-shaped petals of pale blue on plants of willow-shaped leaves. It reaches a height of about 36 inches. Native to the United States, it is pest-free and drought tolerant. Perhaps the best part of amsonia is that while it looks pretty blooming all spring, it looks just as well with its wispy summer foliage and in the fall when its leaves turn bright yellow. It can be used with shrubs as an accent or with other summer flowers like shasta daisy, late-blooming tulips and dusty miller.

Pincushion flower (*Scabiosa*, full sun) are favorites in all my friends' gardens. They grow up to 24 inches tall and are topped all summer with round, lavender-blue blossoms. It is easy to grow in loose, organic soil. A variety called Fama has silvery centers and stamens giving it a pin-cushion appearance. Scabiosa has deeply-divided dark green leaves. It makes the most impact when planted in groups. Try it alongside purple coral bells. They also compliment many shades of pinks, whites and blues.

Of Weeds and Wildflowers
Chicory

One of my most favorite flowers of childhood -- after violets, of course -- was the common chicory (*Cichorium intybus*). In my small town there were numerous open fields and back roads where chicory grew in all its splendor. Today it is hardly seen at all except occasionally in waste places.

I liked the sky-blue flowers with their pinked petal tips, but to pick a bouquet of it for my mother's kitchen table, just couldn't be done. Chicory is as tough and stringy a plant as anyone could ever find, so I would let it stay in its field or roadside place, to admire it there. Amid the blossoms of blue, I could always to find a stray white one or two.

The leaves of this perennial, shaped much like the dandelion and related to it, have been used throughout the centuries as salad greens. In more recent times during two world wars, its roasted roots served as a substitute or addition to coffee.

It has not been used in cultured gardens yet, to my knowlege, for to transplant it from the wild would not be practical at all. It has a tap root that if not dug carefully enough could easily be damaged to the point of not surviving.

This 24-inch high plant puts on its best appearance when colonized, as opposed to having only a few single plants among the prima donnas of a garden.

Unfortunately for this useful, blue-flowering plant, it is declared a noxious weed in Pennsylvania.

Growing the Best Loupes

antaloupes are available year-round at the super market, but the ones you grow are going to be the best ones. The ideal soil for them should contain lots of organic material and be located in a well-drained, sunny spot.

If you grow them (or other squashes) every year, you will eventually encounter squash vine borers. A remedy for borers is given in *Squash, Summer or Winter* in May.

At the beginning of the ripening stage, pick off all the ends of the vines. About 3 weeks later (mark it in your journal) take off all the smaller, green melons, leaving only the ones that will mature before frost. This allows the plant's strength to be used on the fruit that is left. After that, keep any new fuzzy ends that grow picked off.

Sometimes melons from your garden may lack flavor. This could be caused by damage to leaves (disease or hailstones, for example), or they may have been subjected to a heavy water load near the time of harvest.

The question many people have regarding cantaloupes is how to tell when they are ripe. They are at their best when ripened on the vine, not on the kitchen counter. Smell is one indication -- nice, sweet -- but if you can't get your nose down that far to the ground, check the stem where it joins the melon. The most reliable clue is the condition called slip stage. That is when the fruit separates easily from the stem when slight pressure is exerted on the stem by the thumb. Also look for a slight softening at the blossom end.

A friend noticed over the years that when one cantaloupe ripens, they all ripen at the same time. If you could eat them 3 times a day, that still wouldn't reduce the pile of ripened melons waiting in the kitchen. He recommended using a solution he learned from a commercial grower in California. For this method use only ripe melons with no surface blemishes. Fill a large pot with hot water (135 to 140 degrees) and submerge a cantaloupe into it holding it down for 3 minutes. Remove, dry immediately, put in a plastic bag, squeeze out all the air and close tightly with a twist tie. Then refrigerate. The cantaloupes will keep for up to 30 days, he told me. Otherwise, after harvesting, keep them refrigerated until use.

Fresh Garden Pickles

These fresh pickles are easy to do, no preserving necessary. They are a very different type of treat for picnics. As long as the July garden vegetables continue to produce, this recipe works like a charm. I sometimes buy those items that are not available in my garden because of season limitations. Nothing can beat home-grown, garden fresh flavors. These pickles are bound to please.

2 cups whole, fresh, small-sized green beans and/or wax beans
1 ½ cups carrots, cut in 1-inch pieces
½ cup cider vinegar
1/4 cup water
½ fresh red chili pepper, chopped (remove seeds)
2 large garlic cloves, chopped
½ teaspoon salt
1/4 teaspoon crushed, hot red pepper flakes
1 tablespoon dried dill or 1/4 cup fresh dill, snipped small with
        scissors
2 or 3 pickling cucumbers, 4 to 5 inches long cut into spears

Cook beans for 2 minutes. Add carrots and cook 2 minutes longer. Drain, set aside in large bowl.

Combine vinegar, water, chili peppers, chopped garlic, salt and crushed red pepper flakes. Heat to boiling, remove and stir in dill.

Combine cucumber spears with cooked vegetables in bowl. Pour hot vinegar mixture over vegetables and let stand for half hour to cool. Transfer all to a leak-proof plastic bag and marinate in refrigerator up to 4 days. Turn the bag occasionally to fully marinate every vegetable. For my family, which has a big appetite for all things pickled, this makes 8 servings.

Year-Round Color From heathers and heaths

How would you like to have garden plants that offer color year-round, are evergreen, drought-tolerant and need minimal care? Take a look at heathers and heaths. Heath (*Erica spp.*) and heather (*Calluna vulgaris*) are small beauties that fulfill a lot of wishes. Depending on the variety, they bloom nearly all year.

Irish heath (*Daboecia*) is a fine rock-garden plant. It does best in full sun to partial shade. It sets numerous rose-purple, white or rose-pink blossoms from early summer to mid-fall, growing 18 inches high. Some experienced gardeners say that it grows better in Zones 7 or 8 (more southerly), and others state it suits Zone 6. A sheltered spot in your garden may make the difference.

Heathers do the same job that heaths do, but are less shade tolerant. They look best when planted in drifts, massed in large patches, using their complementary foliage or flower colors. Groupings of 5 or more of each color makes an impact, spacing about 12 to 18 inches apart. They take several years to spread to cover the ground in a colorful patchwork.

> *"By choosing specific varieties, it is possible to have bloom for 12 months of the year."*

If mass planting isn't your thing, fewer of them are colorful anywhere. Blossom colors range from pure white through pinks, purples, blues and crimson. Foliage of some is striking, as well, with shades from deep green through gold, to reddish winter tints. Some foliage is gray.

Their planting preferences are for poorer soil, slightly acidic. At planting time dig peat in just to make sure. A mulch of pine bark or pine needles keeps beds weed free until they spread and fill in.

By choosing specific varieties, it is possible to have bloom for 12 months of the year. For instance, *Calluna vulgaris,* June to December; *Erica carnea*, December through May; *Erica cinerea*, June through November. Shop around. Consult catalogs. There may not be the assortment you want right now. It may take several seasons to find them. Planting times for these plants are both spring and fall.

harvesting Tips

You have tended your garden all spring and now comes the part you've been waiting for...the harvest. Ah, this is it. There may be some tips here that can clue you in on whether you've been doing the right things with your garden produce. When are they ripe? When are they over-ripe? I'll tell you how to know.

Beans, snap, green or wax. Pick before the pods show signs of enlarging seeds. They should be straight, slim and will snap when bent.

Carrots. They should be one- or two-inches in diameter depending on what variety you've chosen. Check by unearthing the top of one or two to measure. Danvers, for instance, should be about 2 inches; Nantes, 1 inch.

Cucumbers. Pick when young -- that is, when the little spines are still present along ridges in the skin. Once the spines have smoothed off, it's late. Also some pickling varieties should never grow longer than 4 inches.

Eggplants. Smooth and glossy are the keywords here (see *Eggplant Strategies*, July).

Lettuces. Although many of us harvest the entire plant of leaf lettuces, they can also be harvested by cutting or snapping off the outer leaves.

Onions. When about half of the green tops have dried and drooped down, they are ready to be pulled. Do it when you are expecting several dry, sunny days. Let them dry right on top of the soil after pulling. Then, bring them in for storage.

Peas. Pods should be swelled sufficiently to see the outlines of peas within, and the pods shiny. Refrigerate until ready to cook.

Peas, snow. Pods should be totally flat when picked, not showing enlarged seeds within.

Peppers. For green peppers, check the seed packet or catalog. Some varieties, if left on the plant longer, will ripen into red ones. Skin should be firm and not wrinkled.

Tomatoes. Pick when they are fully red and are still firm. Other colored varieties should also be fully colored, not greenish.

For harvesting other vegetables, read the seed packet or refer to catalogs.

August
Checklist

✔ Keep after those greedy weeds so they won't continue to gobble up the much-needed nutrients and moisture that your more delicate garden plants crave.

✔ Continue adding garden refuse and grass clippings to the compost pile but make sure you are not adding diseased plants or weed seeds.

✔ Too many grass clippings for the compost pile to take all at once? Let them dry a day or two and add a quantity to flower and vegetables beds as a mulch, keeping them away from stems by a couple of inches.

✔ Cut down hollyhock stalks as soon as they have finished blooming.

✔ In cutting gladiolus stalks for indoor arrangements, do not cut off the leaves. These are providing nourishment to the corms.

✔ Ideal temperature ranges for pepper plants is about 70 to 80 degrees F. daytime, and 60 to 75 degrees F. at night. Above and below these temperatures, blossom drop can be expected. If you see this happening during a heat spell, renewed vigor from pepper plants can be seen as soon as the temperatures come within range again.

✔ Worried about an extended drought? Here are several things you can try to invite a rainstorm:

❦ Wash the car.

❦ Hang the laundry out before going away for the day.

❦ Wash the windows and leave them open before going to work.

❦ Plan a big outdoor picnic.

❦ Leave the umbrella at home.

❦ Deep-water your most valuable shrubs.

Any or all of these have been known to bring on rainy weather.

✔ Katydids start singing on August 1. It is reported that the date of their singing is a prediction of the first frost, six weeks hence. It doesn't always work, but to me they herald the end of summer .

✔ Tomato hornworms are active now and so are flea beetles (see *Insect Insights,* August).

✔ When harvesting things like eggplants or peppers, have a paring knife with you, or pruning shears. Just cut them off; don't twist or yank. Your plants will thank you.

✔ Pick zucchinis every day while they're still small whether you want to or not. Finger-length is ideal and a gourmet's delight. Serve them sliced in salads, in strips for dipping or sauted in olive oil with onions and garlic.

✔ We know that once in a while cucumbers and zucchinis can hide in their foliage, escaping your notice, until they are too large to use. By then the seeds have enlarged and become tough. Worst case scenario, they've started turning yellow. Then cut them into chunks and add them to the compost pile.

I remember when daisies and black-eyed Susans grew in every field. How nice to see them perpetuated in gardens now, since paving and building have taken away their original habitats.

Closeup on Clematis

Clematis vines are a long-standing favorite. There are large-blossomed ones of dramatic colors and the old-fashioned, white, C. *maximowicziana*, that blooms in late summer and imparts a heady perfume that neighbors share. This was the one I knew from childhood. The fragrance was at its zenith when I was preparing to go back to school. My nose knew that summer was over.

Clematis vines offer an enormous array of flower colors and have multiple uses in the garden. They can be trained to climb an arbor, trellis, lamppost or wall. If allowed to sprawl, the variety mentioned above (C. *Maximowicziana*) can act as a ground cover.

They should be planted in well-worked soil to which sand and peat have been added, and a handful of lime. Set the plant in the hole and position it about one inch below the soil level when it was in its pot. Some vines come with small trellises about 18 inches high -- just enough for them to start their climb until they reach the bottom rung of your arbor or pergola. If the trellis is not included with your purchase, direct the vine's growth upward by using a stake or two until the plant reaches its permanent support.

Clematis can be planted in spring or fall. Choose a location that receives 5 to 6 hours of sunlight a day. Roots will extend deeply where they can find cool, moist soil. It is a good idea to plant annuals around the base of a clematis or a shrub which help keep the soil and roots cool. Another option is to just use mulch.

Keep your clematis vines well-watered and do not let them dry out. Even when mature, they require a good watering about once a week in dry weather.

Clematis blossoms are large and dramatic, some as big as ten inches across. There is quite an array from which to choose. Will Goodwin (true blue with gold anthers), The President (deep purple, a continuous bloomer), Ramona (lavender-blue with dark anthers), Dr. Ruppel (white with ruffled edges and deep red centers), and Naiobe (very dark ruby red with gold anthers). Every one of these is a winner.

Insect Insights
Tomato Hornworms

A friend said to me incredulously, "Where did the top of my tomato plant go?"
The leaves of the top third were stripped away. This is traumatic if you have just a few plants.

"Tomato hornworm, my dear," I knowingly murmured. We found the green monster hiding in the green foliage and picked it off.

Disposing of such worms is a matter is personal taste. To step on it, ugh, it's so big. Garbage disposal? We couldn't decide. Joe put a rock over it and stamped on the rock. No one in the family went near the spot for days. But the easiest way to dispose of those enormous worms is to drop them into a can of soapy water.

If you have never met a hornworm before, it is fat, green, about 2 to 3 inches long and has a single thorn at the end of its tail. They have been known to consume whole plants in one night. They also like eggplant, pepper and potato plants.

When you see one walking around carrying little white cocoons attached to its back, stand off. It will die very soon of dehydration. The tiny braconid wasp is a predator that uses the worms as an incubator for its eggs. The hatching eggs draw out juices from the worm's body, eventually killing it. Leave it in place to ensure another generation of little wasps to protect the rest of your garden.

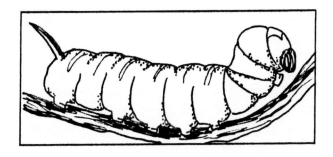

Flea Beetles

While examining plants, you may begin to notice tiny, scatter-shot holes in the leaves of eggplants, cabbages, radishes, beans, tomatoes or peppers. You might even see some of these symptoms on grapes, strawberries and chrysanthemums. Looking further may reveal tiny, shiny, black beetles resting on the leaves, that when approached or disturbed, will hop away like fleas. These beetles are the adults that eat the leaves and will be laying eggs to make more generations of beetles that love being in your garden. They especially love young transplants.

The adults spend the winter under leaves or debris. In the early spring they feed on weeds and foliage of trees until the more tasty plants are available in the garden. Eggs hatch in a week and the larvae feed on roots in the ground for several weeks. Adults emerge to lay their eggs -- the second generation. There are usually 2 generations of flea beetles each summer. That's a lot of flea beetles living in your garden.

The control of these tiny pests is very much the same as used for the control of leaf miners which is discussed in July *Insect Insights*. But there is one more method of control. Apply a band of wood ashes around the stems of the plants *before* they are affected. A band of used coffee grounds also may work. The hard, sharp surfaces of ashes and grounds deter larvae from crawling across to reach the plants.

help! The Aliens have Landed

An alien invasion is taking place but the aliens are not from another planet. The aliens are plants. They have been artificially introduced into a region where they were not known. This introduction could have been accidental or intentional. In regions where aliens appear, native species are being rapidly lost. Aliens are aggressive and invasive, spreading quickly and crowding out the less aggressive native plants. Seed production is typically prolific.

Worse, these alien plants are free of natural controls such as diseases and insects that, in their native habitat, would keep them under control.

Invasives can be trees, vines, flowers, grasses or shrubs and they spread quickly by roots, seeds, shoots or all three. They mature quickly. They are usually colonizers of disturbed ground. Even when planted in your own yard for your own pleasure, it is very possible

they can spread to outlying areas. Then they continue unchecked into farm fields and parks. They are very expensive to control.

This was not a concern when many foreign plants found their way here with explorers, immigrating families or when certain plants were widely advertised as "the newest" to have in a garden. The noxious multiflora rose was touted as a "living hedge" for property or field borders. It quickly got out of control when it seeded itself in grain fields. That grain was used for fodder, causing serious problems for livestock that ate it. Bull thistle has the same reputation.

Believe it or not, some alien invasives are still being sold in nurseries. You will find purple loosestrife and multiflora rose, English ivy, periwinkle and Norway maple.

It is hard to believe that poison ivy is not one of these invasives. It is actually a native of North America and its growth habits do not disrupt nearby vegetation to the point of overtaking it.

If invasives have already taken over an area where you live, it may be necessary to include cutting or pulling those plants as a part of your routine gardening chores. They are listed in the Appendix, *Invasive Plants in Pennsylvania*, made available by the Pennsylvania Department of Conservation and Natural Resources.

Ways to control them is through you. Avoid using known invasives, check your property annually to detect their presence, remove them and replace with native or non-invasive species.

Barking Up A Tree

Bark is the outer skin of a tree. It is woody or corky and dead in appearance, seeming to have no function. However, it is an important protection for the green inner layer known as the cambium. The cambium is very much alive. The bark is the layer of protection for the inner layer that takes foods to the roots that are manufactured in the leaves. Cutting a complete circle around a tree through the cambium layer will ultimately kill it. American Indians knew this well, for they girdled trees in order to kill them for poles. This cambium layer is the origin of the protective scars that form over wounds.

It is important to protect the bark of your trees and shrubs against many enemies, for when the bark is torn or scuffed, it is an attractive place for insects or rot to settle in. Lawn mowers and string weeders are the most common enemies of tree bark. Place a sleeve, like a plastic guard, around the trunk if you know mowing will take place against it. Plastic guards can be bought at most garden stores. Or use a circular mulch bed several feet in diameter surrounding the trunk to preclude any close connection with lawn machinery. Bark mulch of coniferous trees makes a fine substance to use. It repels destructive garden slugs. A layer of only a few inches of mulch will be sufficient (see *Removing the Mystery of Mulch*, April).

> *"Lawn mowers and string weeders are the most common enemies of tree bark."*

Under deep snow mice and moles make tunnels which often lead to their food sources such as tree barks that are also under the snow. Rabbits and other rodents know a delicious tree trunk when they see or smell one. By spring there could have been plenty of nibbling damage done. Before this happens, wrap fine-mesh screening around the trunks, pushing it into the soil just a little and carrying it up a foot or two.

Older trees and shrubs are prone to rot or decay, possibly caused years earlier by damage of some sort. As a general rule, many trees have the ability to heal their own wounds. Play the waiting game and let this happen first instead of applying any substance over a wound.

Tomato TLC

If you like tomatoes (and I know a few who do not) you are probably harvesting those delicious red globes already. Some folks I know have established a ritual regarding tomato harvesting. They take the salt shaker to the garden when the first picking is planned. Then, standing in the hot sun among the tomato plants, they eat the first, sun-warmed red tomato, done to a turn, with a liberal application of salt. This can feel quite close to heaven, they declare.

Keep the water flowing to those plants. Lack of adequate water during dry spells can create a deficiency which causes rot at the blossom end, aptly known as blossom end rot. If the situation is corrected by watering, sometimes the plant can grow out of it. When watering, try not to wet the leaves. Wet leaves make high humidity among plants and can create a perfect climate for fungus diseases. As a guideline for watering, I would suggest that each tomato plant needs about 2 ½ gallons per week from flowering time through harvest time. See *Have a Drink*, July, for additional watering tips. A rain gauge is helpful to measure approximately how much moisture is coming from rain. It can allow you to add the balance that nature doesn't provide. Mulch does help retain moisture. That is a good reason to mulch with any organic materials you have such as compost or grass clippings. The object is to avoid the alternating dry-wet sequences that create plant stress.

When plants are crowded (putting in more than *really* intended because the market packs had 8 plants and there was room for only 6), it makes a perfect set up for fungal development. Next year, give away those extras or close your eyes while you drop them onto the compost pile. Don't talk to them or you'll become attached.

While anticipating those red, red tomatoes, treat yourself to a couple of green ones -- you know, like fried green tomatoes.

My recipe is simple. Slice the greenies about 1/4 inch thick and dip in flour or cornmeal. Fry several minutes on one side; turn and do the other side. They are extra good with a slice or two of bacon for breakfast, or as a side dish for any meal.

Begonias, Not Strawberries

Alittle-known plant that is a gem for every shady garden is the strawberry begonia (*Saxifraga stolonifera*). It is also called mother-of-thousands because of the way it reproduces. Another common name is strawberry geranium because its small leaves resemble those of the geranium.

This hardy little begonia does extremely well, year-round, in our temperate zone, although it is grown more widely below the Mason Dixon Line.

It has many things going for it. It is an elegant, perennial ground cover. It sports smallish, round, silver-veined leaves. Characteristically, it grows only a few inches high, sending up flower stalks in the spring with lacy flowers of pink or white. The flower stalks become brown and shaggy after blooming, so I use kitchen scissors to snip them off, leaving only the low-growing leaves. It will reproduce itself with thread-like stolons, or runners, just like strawberries, and it is virtually evergreen, forming thick patches that defy weeds.

> "*It is virtually evergreen forming thick patches that defy weeds.*"

This hardy begonia is well-adapted to growing in retaining walls, paving and crevices, and in rock gardens.

As a houseplant, it is well-behaved, never getting too big to handle. Just as the spider plant does, it sends out stolons to make new babies that trail over the edge of the pot. This adds to its attractive quality.

It is so compact that it can be used as a ground cover in a larger pot that might house a palm or other tall, low-light plant. As if this were not enough, it can be used in dish gardens and in terrariums, since it doesn't overwhelm as it grows.

It is not commonly shown in catalogs, but a complete garden store will carry pots of it in the spring.

Try strawberry begonia as either a houseplant or as a permanent resident in your garden. It is likely to exceed your expectations.

Earthworms

I found a gold mine of humus when I did some summer clearing. One hundred years ago it was an area that had been a repository for stray stones from a pasture. Over time, autumn leaves fell there to lay and decompose. When I removed the stones and a few weeds, I found an 8-inch-deep layer of humus and plenty of wiggling, red earthworms.

I usually distribute the wealth of worms that I find by adding some to the compost pile and putting some into the garden. A worm, though, usually will not thrive if its habitat is changed from where it started unless the new habitat is of a very similar composition.

Earthworms are beneficials. They travel down to depths of over 4 feet. Their networks of tunnels aerate the soil, increasing water absorption and allowing plant roots to spread. Their castings are a rich manure and become part of the soil, adding nutrients such as nitrogen, phosphorous and potash. Earthworms are virtually miniature compost factories.

They should be a healthy red color and be active when disturbed. If pale and sluggish, do them and your garden a favor by adding a lot of organic material to the soil. The worms will get to work on it, transforming that material into a form that your plants can use and the worms will be nourished, as well.

That childhood tale that a severed worm will produce 2 worms, is not factual. A worm can regenerate itself from the top down if the cut is not too high or if the sever is not too torn.

If you are concerned about harming them when digging, dig in the middle of the day at which time they have burrowed deeply into the ground, or use a garden fork instead of a shovel or spade.

In recent years another specie of earthworm has invaded sections of the country. They are the ones used by fisherman, who at the end of the day, discard unused worms on stream banks. These fishing worms are much larger than the common ones and do no harm in gardens, but their appetite for leaf litter is enormous. Enormous to such an extent that, in forests, they are a threat to healthy soil structure and the forests themselves. Presently there is no conceivable remedy, so we have to become accustomed to their presence until we find a protection for forested areas.

Rainy Day Quiz

How savvy are you regarding garden pests and diseases? It always helps to be well-informed.

1. What is the first step in combatting any garden pest or disease?

2. Your garden space measurements allow room for only 6 new market pack plants. Why shouldn't you squeeze in 2 more if the market pack comes with 8 plants in it?

3. Why shouldn't you water the garden in the evenings? It seems like such a nice time of day to do it.

4. Can your choices of what you wear and what you eat attract the wrong kind of friends at a family picnic?

Answers

1. Early observation. In visiting your gardens every day or every-other day, you will often notice if changes are taking place. When a change involves a new insect or disease, it is much easier to control in the early stages.

2. Overcrowding produces weak plants. It creates too much competition for moisture and sunlight. Crowding invites insect and fungal attacks by hampering air circulation.

3. Watering the soil in the evenings is all right to do by trickling or by soaker hose, but only if you *do not wet the whole plant*. Leaves left wet overnight sets up a prime situation for fungal infections to get started.

4. Don't make friends with a mosquito. They just love the color blue more than any other color. To make matters worse for you, don't be found eating bananas outside, because they love them, too.

herb of the Month
Lovely Lavender

The fragrance of lavender can immediately transport one to other places and other times. It is used in cosmetic formulas and pot pourri. For an attractive sachet, tie its leaves inside a pretty handkerchief with a ribbon. Tie a bundle of long stems of blossoms or buds around the middle to lay on a window sill. The warm sunlight will release the fragrance.

In the garden, it forms showy flower spikes that rise above a mound of silver-grey leaves. It will be in flower throughout early summer. Lavender does its best in a full-sun location. When grown as hedges it is stunning to see in bloom.

The seeds of this plant have a long germination period and are difficult to get started. It is less stressful to buy plants in pots. When shopping, there will be many varieties from which to choose. Be prepared to know how much space there is for them and read the labels for the height and width that each mature plant will become.

It can be effective as a container plant but a little temperamental to keep indoors in the winter, since it thrives in a nighttime temperature range of 40 to 50 degrees and daytime only 10 degrees higher. The potted plant needs a very sunny spot to do well, and can be let to go dry between waterings.

Lavender has a tendency to sprawl and get leggy, so pruning will keep it compact. Remove dead flower stems and about an inch or two of top leaf growth to form a rounded shape.

Harvest the blossom stems for drying either just when the buds open or when they are in full bloom.

Lavendula augustifolia "Munstead" offers lavender or lilac flower spikes over a long season and is very fragrant. Its height reaches about 15 inches. "Hidcote" is the deepest purple-blue of all the lavenders. Its mounded leaves are a silver-green and reaches only about 12 inches, making it an excellent choice as a dwarf hedge. "Rosea" produces pink flowers, and other varieties come in white.

It has some culinary uses as well. See *Lavender Lemonade* in the June section of this book and *Stop and Eat the Flowers* in July.

Of Weeds and Wildflowers
Day lily

Roadside day lilies (*Hemerocallis fulva*) are at their peak in mid-summer, cheering your way as you drive by. The common orange day lily, however, is considered by most naturalists to be an alien invasive and one that should be removed from the countryside.

True, they do form thick patches that expand in size each year, crowding out less robust natives. In bloom they are a joy to see, but if possible, their clumps should be kept in check. The two clumps in my own yard are kept limited in size and enjoyed. They spread not by seeds, but by their expanding, tuberous roots.

Blossoms last only one day, hence the name, opening in the mornings and expiring by nightfall. When cutting for wildflower arrangements, we are often disappointed that by evening the open blossoms are folding. But there is a succession of blooms for each day as more buds on the stalk come to maturity.

The plants, originally from Asia, have acclimated well to our climate and have spread in moist, sunny roadsides.

They are easily transplanted by dividing the roots of old clumps in the autumn.

Day lilies have never been used medicinally, but their buds and flowers can be used for food. (See *Stop and Eat the Flowers*, July.) Their tubers can be eaten raw or roasted, and have a nut-like flavor.

Plant breeders have hybridized these oriental day lilies and have succeeded in creating blossoms that will last for almost a week instead the one-day habit of the originals.

Egyptian Onions

Egyptian onions have been part of the human diet for thousands of years. Yet many gardeners today have not discovered their benefits. They are an heirloom vegetable and once planted, will endure permanently, being very cold and heat tolerant. While fertilizing is not necessary, they will respond well to an occasional application of a general, all-purpose fertilizer.

Settlers in this country brought them from the homeland and early German immigrants in this region commonly grew them in their kitchen gardens for year-round use. In January or February snow, their sturdy, green sprouts can be uncovered and used.

They have many names, variously called multiplying, circle, walking, top-set, or winter onions. Ungainly in appearance, they do not belong in an ornamental bed.

With so many names attached to this onion, what can it possibly look like? An explanation of its life cycle can enlighten.

Planting the bulblets in August or September is the first step. Sink them into the ground just to cover. By early spring, sprouts appear as scallions and can be used as such, being careful to leave a quantity in the soil for maturing.

As the season progresses, the green stalks grow quite tall, are hollow, and by mid-summer get twisty, little knots at the tops, containing a cluster of new "sets" or bulblets. Growing out of these clusters, smaller twisty stems can appear with smaller sets at the tips. (Hence, one of its names, top-set.) They are curious enough in appearance to include in flower arrangements for their unusual shapes and purple-hued skins.

As the sets mature and the stalks turn brown, the plant collapses and falls where the sets take root forming next year's crop. If left exactly where they drop, they will grow in a circle pattern, hence one of its other names, circle onion.

Throughout the spring, summer and fall these onion plants can be harvested as needed. The tough stalks can be cut crosswise to include in soups and stews. Roots themselves can also be used and when the sets form at the top, they too can be peeled and added to any meat or vegetable dish, whole or diced. The flavor is stronger than common yellow onions, so they can be conserved by using sparingly and can also be used as a substitute for shallots.

Neighbors who grow this variety often share their bulblets or sets with others, but if there is no local source available, check Nichols Garden Nursery listed in the January section of this book.

Fertilizing Technique: Adding fertilizer to a dry soil -- either to plants in the ground or to those in flower pots -- can sometimes cause a root-burn condition. Fertilize after a rain or a watering so the uptake action of the roots is somewhat diluted and can carry the fertilizer along through the plant's system without shock.

With a Passion
Summer Passion Salad

While the bounty of gardens is pouring in, we try to take advantage of all that good, fresh food. If you are as passionate about your vegetables as my family is, you will love this salad.

I found it years ago and it instantly became a family hit. It is simple to fix, and is so filling, it goes a long way at the table. All of the ingredients have come from my garden. This can be served with only a crusty bread. If more substance is needed, a chop, grilled chicken or browned sausage goes well with it.

Passion Salad

Fresh tomatoes, cut into wedges
Potatoes, boiled and cut into 1-inch cubes
Green beans, cooked only about 2 or 3 minutes
Red onion, sliced.

Green beans comprise about half of the salad volume. Equal portions of the tomatoes and potatoes make up the rest. Add onions to taste. (Vegetable portions can be adjusted to family's likes.)

Dressing: 3 parts olive oil, 1 part red wine vinegar, salt and pepper to taste. Toss and serve.

A friend remarked, "Remember when we were kids, canned green beans accompanied every meal? After they came out of the can, they were cooked again on the stove. No wonder I grew up thinking green beans were brown."

Checklist

✔ Some perennials may have outgrown the spaces that you have allotted for them. Now is a good time to divide them and get the new divisions established before frost. The other optimum time for dividing will be in the early spring.

✔ Lily of the valley beds that have become crowded or have expanded their territory can be thinned. My lilies sprout up in the middle of a gravel path. These are either removed and given to friends, or composted.

✔ Your lawn might not be at its very best at this season, but right now is an excellent time to sow grass seed to fill in bare spots in well-used areas. You will see the benefits early next spring in an already established turf. Keep the seeds and new grass watered until frost.

✔ Enjoy your garden blossoms while you can, bringing cut flowers into the house to enjoy for a short time longer.

✔ Although competition for nutrients between garden plants and weeds is greatly diminished now, it will pay to keep pulling those weeds no matter how innocent they appear to be, and no matter how depleted your garden is from seasonal harvests. Those little weeds have seeds on them, so out they go, fast.

✔ One little crabgrass plant that you don't pull now will produce hundreds of seeds, all waiting to sprout next spring.

✔ Many garden centers have seasonal sales of perennials. Look them over. Undoubtedly, there are some you would like to add to your gardens. They will have time to get roots established before frost comes next month.

✔ September and October are good months to look at fruit tree selections. They can be planted as late as November. However, it is best to put in peaches, plums and cherries in the spring. Make sure your new trees will be situated in full sun and in compost-rich, well-drained soil. (See *Fruit Tree Tips*, September.)

✔ This old adage warns, "Thunder in September brings plenty of snow in February." I do not know the source of this, but take note. We will find out if this is true. Just in case, get the firewood contact made and the chimney swept.

✔ Plant garlic now. Work compost into the soil making it loose and light. Remove the brittle skin of grocery store garlic cloves, set each clove upright about a half-inch deep and about 5 inches apart. Let them develop over the winter.

✔ Compost Reminder: When using compost in your beds, use only the finely decomposed material, because stuff that hasn't finished decomposing yet *can* burn plants.

✔ Keep removing spent leaves and stalks in the garden. Insects take refuge in them and happily over-winter there. Don't make it easy for them.

✔ In the vegetable bed, if there is a plant that has not quite made the grade all summer, away with it! It's not likely to produce anything now.

✔ September is probably the last month of the year in which grass cutting is still necessary on a regular basis. Grass clippings can still be used as a mulch on beds, just remember to keep them about an inch or two away from plant stems. Over the next season, they will gradually compost, improving your soil.

✔ The gladiolus in your garden are still blooming beautifully. Before the soil freezes, lift the corms, brush off the soil and let them dry for a few days. Cut the leaves down to about 2 inches and store them in a cool, ventilated area for the winter.

> *The very last of sweet corn is still available. Don't forget all those husks and corn cobs can be added to the compost pile.*

house Plant Vacation
is Over

House plants have benefitted from their summer vacation outside. The fun's over. In September, they should be cleaned up and moved indoors until next year. With the abundance of summer light, humidity and regular fertilizing they put out new growth. They will still benefit from mild, sunny days of September, but by the end of the month, they should be safely indoors, away from those increasingly chilly nights.

Houseplants that have spent the summer outside need to be checked carefully for insects that have harbored in them. Place each pot in the sink, or do this in a bucket. Flood each pot to the brim. Worms that

> *"In September, they should be cleaned up and moved indoors until next year."*

have worked their way into the pot will come to the surface and can be tipped away. Examine for spiders, cobwebs or any condition that suggests insects. Spray the whole plant, including undersides of leaves, with tepid water to rinse off hitch-hikers like red spider mites. Other sucking insects can be read about in *Insect Insights* for March.

A spray of an insecticidal soap will help remove any transients coming inside with your houseplants.

Should you fertilize these plants that are going to spend the winter inside? The whole matter depends on the amount of light they will receive. Herbs, for instance, that will be placed in a very bright, sunny window will benefit from feeding. Fertilizers act in combination with soil and light. In the winter, greatly reduced light makes the fertilizer crystallize in the soil and on the pot, creating a condition detrimental to the plant. In this case, wait until the longer, sunnier days of late March to start a fertilizing routine.

Fruit Tree Tips

Picking fruit right off the backyard tree makes fine eating; apples, cooled and crisped in the autumn air, sweetened to perfection, are worth growing.

Dwarf trees are traditionally the most popular family fruit tree for several reasons. They do not require a lot of room, they produce fruit usually during the second year, and their fruit size is as large as any from a standard tree. Because of the dwarfed size, picking fruits and pruning can be handled without ladders.

There is one drawback. Deer eat everything they can reach. A standard-sized tree is a better solution in that case. A long-handled picker works fine for high branches and a pressure sprayer shoots far at spraying time.

In this region, autumn is the best time to plant new trees; spring is second choice. In early to mid-autumn, there is still time before freezing weather for new tree roots to become established. Believe it or not, the winter's alternating freezes and thaws can help settle roots. Planting instructions come with every tree, but here are some extra tips.

They require full sun and a place with good drainage. What consists of good drainage? In many places, there is a deep layer of clay beneath the topsoil. If that is a problem in your yard, dig a large hole 2 or 3 days before planting. Pour in a bucket of water. If it doesn't drain out in a day, dig it another foot deeper. Add stones to the bottom then add good soil and compost. Plant as usual. Another option is to try a few other sites, but the clay is likely to be widespread.

Once a young tree is in the ground, it can be staked to keep it in place during very wet or windy weather.

The tender bark on your new tree will be just what hungry mice and rabbits will long to taste during the winter months. Protect against this kind of damage. Wrap the trunk in 1/4 inch hardware mesh, extending it slightly into the soil and up to the lower branches. Other rodent-proof wraps are available at garden stores, so there will be a selection from which to choose.

Mulching is useful during the growing season for many reasons. This is explained in *Removing the Mystery of Mulch*, April.

hollies

Hollies (*Ilex species*) are among the most popular ornamental shrubs. There are over 500 varieties, 19 of which are native to the United States. Since ancient times, the word holly has been synonomous with the holiday season. Druids considered it a "holy" plant, which may be the source of its common name.

There are both evergreen and deciduous hollies -- the deciduous being known as winterberry.

Mature holly trees can add value to a property. Few plants are as easy to grow, for they are tolerant of a variety of soils and require minimum care, except for feeding and watering.

In order for berries to be produced, it is necessary to have both a male and female plant. The word for this is dioecious. It means male and female flowers are on separate plants. Only the females produce berries, but both males and females produce flowers. If you want several that will produce berries, have one male closeby, but if it is in too distant a location or around a corner of the house, pollination may not take place as fully as you'd like. When buying several, make sure that both male and female are of the same variety, such as Blue Prince or Jersey Knight, because you will want the time of blossoming to be exactly the same. Information tags should be attached to each plant.

Buy from a reputable dealer. Large department or home equipment stores will have hollies at very good prices, but you will never know if the tags were properly applied. A nurseryman wouldn't let that happen.

Holly trees do well in full sun as well as half shade. They require acid soil and acid fertilizer. Spring planting is probably the best time to start new plants, but autumn runs a close second with its moist air and mild temperatures. It may be several years before you can harvest berried branches, since the trees should be allowed to grow before cutting.

When planting, prepare the hole by digging twice the size of the rootball. Add compost plus a conditioner such as construction sand to increase aeration. Tamp the soil around the plant and mulch. Remember to water well for the first year and especially during dry spells. For established hollies, fertilize with an organic product that is made especially for acid-loving plants.

The Saffron Crocus

Perhaps you have been surprised by seeing purple crocuses blooming right now. These are not the same ones that are seen the the spring, but the saffron crocus (*Crocus sativus*), an autumn-blooming variety.

In the Middle Ages it was a valuable commodity and was grown commercially. Saffron was traded throughout Europe and India for dyes, food flavoring and medicine. Saffron came to this country with the Schewnkfelders who immigrated from Silesia. They grew it commercially there, and introduced it into their Pennsylvania gardens for home use. It is still grown today for the thread-like, bright red-orange stigmas that are contained in each blossom. Saffron spice can be found in many Pennsylvania groceries today, sold in very small packages as a culinary treat.

> *"This could be your own little culinary sideline, if you wish to grow saffron."*

In using the stigmas, they are steeped in a hot liquid for about 20 minutes, then the liquid is added to the batter. The liquid is used in Pennsylvania Dutch chicken pot pie to create a richer coloring and flavor. It is used in chicken soup, in potato filling and in the well-known Schwenkfelder cake of this region. In some crumb cakes, the steeped threads are included in the crumb topping.

Saffron bulbs are available in some bulb catalogs and specialty greenhouses. They are planted in the autumn, but may not flower until the following fall. Once established, you will find that they will multiply rapidly.

Try harvesting your own saffron. Do this on a sunny morning when the blossoms are open. Carefully pick the stigmas out of each blossom, using tweezers to prevent damage. Dry the stigmas, or threads, and store in a closed container until needed for cooking.

It takes hundreds of flowers to produce an amount that can be marketed, but in the home garden, only about a dozen bulbs will produce enough threads for just a couple of remarkably delicious dishes.

Division of bulbs should take place after about 4 or 5 years in order to prevent crowding and dwindling flower production. This could be your own little culinary sideline.

Plant saffron bulbs in September or early October. Give them a well-drained spot about 4 inches deep and 4 inches apart. If mice or gophers are a problem, plant them in plastic berry boxes or wire mesh.

The leaves, when they first appear, will be grass-like and may be mistakenly cut, so it is important that the saffron crocus bed be marked in some way.

In 1971, The Goschenhoppen Historians (Green Lane, PA) published a manuscript recipe for Schwenkfelder Saffron Cake in their Folk Festival Cook Book. It is a traditional Pennsylvania German "receipt." It came to us from a long-time resident of the area, Sadie Kriebel.

Try this recipe with your first saffron harvest, and have fun looking for more recipes that include this unique spice.

Schwenkfelder Saffron Cake

1 cup mashed potato
½ cup granulated sugar
1 pkg granular yeast
1 cup potato water (water in which the potatoes were boiled.)
1/4 tsp saffron
1/4 cup boiling water
1 cup milk
½ cup shortening
2 eggs
1 cup granulated sugar
½ tsp salt
about 8 cups bread flour

Crumbs: Mix well with hands: 2 cups light brown sugar, 2 ½ cups flour, 1 tsp cinnamon, saffron (the steeped saffron threads), 1 cup shortening.

Thoroughly mix potatoes and ½ cup sugar. Dissolve yeast in lukewarm potato water, add to potato and sugar mixture when lukewarm, cover, let set in warm place about 3 hours.

Put boiling water on saffron to draw out color and flavor.

Bring milk to a boil, add shortening, well-beaten eggs, sugar and salt.

Carefully drain saffron water into this mixture (save the saffron threads for the crumbs) when this is lukewarm, add the yeast mixture and 4 cups flour. Beat well. Cover and let rise until bubbly from 1 to 1 ½ hours. Add rest of flour or enough to make a dough that can be kneaded until smooth. Place in greased bowl, cover and raise about 4 hours or until double in bulk and light.

Roll about ½ inch thick, place on greased cookie sheets or baking pans. Brush top with either melted butter, cream or beaten egg. Cover with crumbs. Let raise about 1 hour. Bake 325 degrees about 20-25 minutes.

Makes four 9-inch cakes.

Sadie Kriebel

Insect Insights
Taking Care of Beneficials

There are good insects and bad ones, and the sooner we learn who the goodies are and who the others are, the better off we will be. When we apply a dose of insecticide to combat a few baddies, we also kill the goodies. That doesn't make sense, because the goodies are supposed to win!

Keeping the garden healthy is the first step. Good rules to follow for the health of your garden would be:

☞ Choose plants that are ideal for your own region, yard and garden.

☞ Keep adding compost and lots of organic materials to the soil.

☞ In dry spells, water.

☞ Practice good housekeeping methods by composting or trashing (at the curb) left-over debris so it doesn't accumulate.

☞ Keep adding notations to your garden journal.

These are all common sense suggestions. Now on to the bugs.

Many beneficial insects are not often seen, but be assured they are there, standing duty for you and for their next meal. These are lady bugs, parasitic wasps, ground beetles, soldier bugs, lacewings, praying mantises, parasitic nematodes, assassin bugs and even flies. Lots more are working in your behalf.

There are ways to attract beneficials. A birdbath in the garden is a place for insects, as well as birds, to take a pause that refreshes. Change water often so stagnation doesn't make it a place to harbor mosquito larvae. Plant flowers that produce pollen or nectar. Attract frogs and toads with toad huts. (See *Leaping Lizards,* June.)

It is possible to buy batches of beneficials by catalog, but frankly, when added to your garden will they stay where they are placed? Chances are, they may leave your garden for places unknown. Others are reliable only if distributed in very large numbers. Aphid midges can be bought, but when aphids first appear in your garden, isn't it simpler to wash them off with a strong spray from the hose? Once knocked off, they don't return.

As they say, "It's a jungle out there," but if you stay on top of conditions, the jungle becomes more friendly.

Mint Teas

Sooner or later, everyone who gardens will have added mint to their collection of plants. It doesn't stop at just one variety. There are dozens from which to choose.

All mints have a way of taking over. Very pushy, I would say. Since they seem to be happy wherever they grow, they will spread by underground runners and will come up in places you wish they wouldn't. They can be contained somewhat by giving them their own planter or by sinking clay flue pipes into the ground for them.

Since they are so exuberant, take advantage of their good nature. As long as the weather allows, collect the leaves to use fresh, and dry as many as you can for some really nice beverages during the winter.

> *"Mints are the perfect beverage plants..."*

For a good iced mint tea, use the following proportions. To make one quart, use 3 tablespoons of fresh leaves or 2 tablespoons of dried. Bring one quart of water to a boil and pour into a warmed china or pottery tea pot. Toss in the fresh or dried mint and let steep 5 or 6 minutes. Steep dried mints a minute longer than fresh. Strain, removing the leaves to prevent bitterness. Cool and serve over ice cubes. Use a fresh mint sprig for garnish or lemon slice.

For hot mint tea, use only 2 tablespoons of fresh leaves or 1 tablespoon of dried to a quart of boiling water. Use peppermint, fresh or dried, in the same proportions. Mint teas can be frozen into ice cubes and added to regular tea for flavorings.

For a different variety, try any of the flavored garden mints or a combination of several to see how you like them. Combine spearmint and lemon balm, or lemon balm with lemon verbena and lemon grass. (See *Herb of the Month: Lemon Balm,* February.)

Pick leaves and sprigs from your plants in the morning after the dew has dried and never pick from plants that have been sprayed. Wash carefully, discarding damaged leaves. Air dry in single layers on a baking sheet.

Mints are the perfect beverage plants, used either hot or cold.

Mum's the Word

There may be a few bare spots in your flower beds at this time of year because some of the flowering plants have just about finished their job for the season. Cheer things up with a number of those wonderful garden mums that are seen in every garden center. The color choices are endless. Among the bright yellows, bronzes, crimsons and golds, can be found apricot, pink, mauve, ivory and white.

Chrysanthemums (*Chrysanthemum*) are the perfect filler for gardens that are at this time of year, lean of color. These bright mums are perfect companions to pumpkins, corn stalks and bales of straw. They are of hardy stock that will weather the winter and come back next year to do a different sort of job by filling in with green foliage until they start blooming at the end of August. They will become leggy unless they are pinched back on a regular basis.

> *"Bright mums are the perfect companions to pumpkins, corn stalks and bales of straw."*

My aunt would scold me for not pinching back my mums. She did hers in late June, then 2 or 3 weeks later, and the last pinching by the end of July. The first one was to reduce the plant by half its height. The last two times, by about 2 inches. Following this routine, they should look approximately like they did when first bought.

Most of the fun of shopping for mums is choosing the colors. I could stand at a display of 200 mums for a half-hour before I could decide what I'd want the colors to do in my garden. An assortment of the lightest and brightest colors would please, highlighted by one or 2 white ones. Picture a combination of deeper-toned ones, accented by one or two very light-shaded ones.

After bringing them home, slip them out of the pots they came in, and plant in holes that were prepared with soil and compost. Keep them watered. They will become a permanent part of your garden. But if you prefer, pull them out after freezing weather kills the tops. Then buy new ones next September.

herb of the Month
Sage

Almost everyone grows sage (*Salvia officinalis*).
Although it is hardy in Zone 6, it has a short life, requiring replacement every 3 or 4 years. Its blue-violet blossoms attract bees that pollinate blooming plants nearby. I have always added sage to the vegetable garden for the pollination benefits. Hummingbirds also find its flowers very attractive.

Like many herbs, it has an ancient history. Used by Romans and Greeks, it flavored many foods. The Chinese favored it as a tea. Other peoples found it suited them best for medicinal use. Surprisingly, worldwide, it has been convenient as a leafy, disposable toothbrush.

Purple sage (*S. officinalis purpurascens*) is the preferred variety for medicinal use. Tea of purple sage has been popular to soothe sore throats and coughs because of its astringent and antiseptic qualities. The leaves may be rubbed on the skin to calm stings and bug bites.

The more popular culinary variety that we grow today (*S. officinalis*), is the one we think of first when considering the Thanksgiving turkey and seasoned sausage. The blossoms of any variety of sage can be used to garnish fruit salads and are, of course, edible.

There are dozens of varieties, but compared to the *officinalis*, they are primarily best at decorating herbal wreaths, offering diversity of foliage to garden beds and for use in flower arrangements.

An exception is the "Albaflora," a white-flowering variety, which is an excellent culinary sage. Other varieties display variegated leaves that have markings in yellow or grey-purple. These are all very attractive to grow and will impart the sage flavor to foods, although less pronounced than the *officinalis*.

Harvest the leaves in the spring before the plant comes to flower, and take from only the upper third of the plant. Harvest can be done again this month. Do it in the morning after the dew has dried. The leaves can be dried on a screen or cookie sheet in a warm, dry place. Jar tightly for use throughout the year.

Dry Your Own Flowers

Cooler days and nights of September make our plants feel as energetic as we do, now that debilitating heat of summer is behind us.

This is a good time to dry some of the last blossoms of summer to include in dry arrangements.

Among the everlastings, hydrangea air-dries beautifully, as do goldenrod (pick when buds are not quite fully open), statice, yarrow, globe thistle (pick while still in bud), straw flowers, pearly everlastings and cockscomb. Also, cut stems of poppy seed pods, bittersweet and rose hips. Experiment with what you have. Don't feel limited to only those listed here.

Air-drying is started by cutting stems, stripping off leaves and hanging them upside down in a warm, dry place such as an attic where there is still ample room for some air circulation. A garage or barn may be

> *"This will be a good time to dry some of the last blossoms of summer..."*

too humid and cause mildew to form. Stems may be sturdy enough not to be wired, but if necessary, wrap stems with green florist tape to strengthen.

Chemical drying is more complex but certainly worth a try. A silica gel is included in flower-drying kits that are sold in craft stores, or you may use 4 parts white cornmeal and one part borax to achieve the same result. Another formula for drying is a mixture of 1 part plain, salt-free, fine sand with 2 parts borax. These mixtures can be re-used year after year. Experiment with different formulas to see which work best for you and for the flowers you choose.

Prepare the flower by removing the stem. Insert a florist wire into the bottom of the blossom, making it poke through the center of the face. Bend it over a half-inch and pull it back into the blossom. Single-blossomed stems such as daisy, zinnia or pansy work well.

Place an inch of the drying-mixture in a small box and insert the flower head into mixture, gently but totally covering the entire blossom. Seal box with a lid to keep out moisture. In 2 weeks, gently remove your dried, but dusty flower. A soft artist's brush removes the excess media. The wire can now be wrapped with green floral tape to replicate a stem and be flexible to use in arrangements.

Glycerine is another media used chiefly for preserving foliage, allowing retention of flexibility in arrangements. Coloring changes occur, sometimes resulting in golden, creamy, brown or dark red or black shades. While leaves are still green, take cuttings of not more than 18 inches in length, and crush the cut ends. Place them in a solution of 1/3 water, 2/3 glycerine, about 4 inches deep, and allow time for the stems to absorb the liquid. Complete absorption may take several days up to a week or two. Any foliage is adaptable, such as magnolia, rhododendron, holly, laurel, boxwood, pachysandra, azalea. Beech leaves take several days to become a tan or brown color. When the upper leaves of the cuttings become the same shade as the lower leaves, it is time to remove them from the glycerine solution. Heavy-leaved cuttings from magnolia, aucuba or rhododendron may take as long as 2 or 3 weeks.

> *Hydrangea Wreath*
> *Tree hydrangeas produce beautiful blooms.*
> *Follow directions for air-drying. Then*
> *separate clusters of the blooms and pin*
> *each small cluster with bent wire pins onto*
> *a straw wreath. Fill the entire wreath with*
> *the exception of the back. Use a velvet*
> *ribbon in pale green or pale rose, leaving*
> *flowing streamers.*

Of Weeds and Wildflowers
Milkweed

The common milkweed (*Asclepias syriaca*) was once a familiar friend to every child who ever romped in fields or along country roadsides. In the spring milkweed sprouted with large, simple leaves. The tops of each stalk soon bloomed with several clusters of small blossoms in a color that is difficult to describe. They could have been pink, or mauve, or pink-brown, or purple-rose. No matter, we searched the colonies of milkweed for the soldier bugs that we always found there. We called them "singing" bugs because, if carefully picked off their sweet blossoms and held between 2 small, cupped hands, the bugs could be heard to sing in a steady, high-pitched cricket song. This never failed to delight us.

Hummingbirds and butterflies are drawn to the fragrant flowers. The plant is related to butterfly weed. The stalks and leaves of milkweed have short hairs that prevent many unwinged insects from climbing them. Animals will not graze on them because of the bitter, sticky, white sap. The sap resembles milk, hence, the name, milkweed. They are perennial and may be grown in a garden as a wildflower if placed in full sun.

The pods are green and warty and hang at odd angles from the stalk tops. When suitably dry, they turn brown and split open, yielding a huge number of seeds and white fluff.

The seeds, similar to dandelion seeds, drift aloft on their silky sails, floating for days before coming back to earth, where they will take root and form another colony. The empty pods continue to dry to a brown-grey with a pearly inner lining that are often collected for craft projects.

Milkweed sap was used medicinally. It served as an early band-aid. Once the sap was applied to a small cut or wound, it would dry, sealing it against infection.

During World War II, milkweed fluff was collected for use in life jackets, being a substitute for the Asian kapok. In the seventeenth and eighteenth centuries the young shoots were cut for table food.

Milkweed has had many, many household uses over the ages. Perhaps there's room somewhere in your garden for it.

Perpetuating Bloomin' Geraniums

The common garden geranium is known as a tender perennial that, in Zone 6, will not survive a winter outdoors. Do you want to keep alive those geraniums that have done so well all summer? Try bringing them into the house.

Give them only minimal care. When the late, bright days of winter come, they will have started new growth and started blooming again. They will be ready to continue blooming when you place them outside in May. What more could you ask of a geranium? Exercise your green thumb and save yourself from more geranium purchases next spring.

> *"...if you are willing to try out your green thumb, plus save yourself from more geranium purchases next spring, this is worth a try."*

Before frost, lift the plants out of the soil. Prune back the tops by about half, remove any long, rangy branches and straggly roots. Cover the hole (or holes) in the bottom of a pot with something like broken pottery or eggshells. A 4-inch pot should be large enough for a mature plant. Use a mixture of 3 parts garden soil, one part peat and one part sand. Geraniums do not need rich soil. If the garden soil is part clay, this will be fine. Water thoroughly to settle the soil around the roots. Don't water again until the surface feels dry.

Now they may be kept in a basement or cellar, as long as they won't freeze. Water occasionally to prevent total drying out.

About the end of January, find a warm, sunny window sill for them and you will be rewarded with new growth and new flower buds. Provide a little fertilizer at this time that is low in nitrogen, such as 5-10-10 and watch those bloomin' geraniums go.

> *"A flower has to go through a lot of dirt before it can bloom."* From *Voice of Health Magazone*

Moles, Voles, What's the Difference?

What is it in your garden that is causing such havoc? Soft spots in the soil emerge and plants disappear. You probably have moles or voles, both of which do considerable damage because of their tunneling habits.

If by chance you see a mole, you would notice that it looks like a fat mouse but with a very long, pink, hairless snout, broad paws with long, paddle-like claws for digging, and grey fur on its body. Eyes are very small and it has no ears. But you probably won't ever see one. They live underground in extensive tunnels and rooms. They are actually doing you a favor by being there, for moles tunnel where they can find food. Their meals consist of many plant pests such a Japanese beetle grubs, cutworms, wireworms, other larvae, and yes, they do eat earthworms when other more delicious foods get scarce. You may find frequent piles of earth like little volcanoes on the ground where their tunnels end or join (known as the proverbial mole hills). Removing the source of food (grubs, larvae) for moles is a preventative by applying milky disease spores to your lawn. Once you destroy the pests that they eat, they will leave.

> *Moles eat grubs and larvae in the soil.*
> *Voles are vegetarians, seeking out your plants to eat.*

Where do voles come into this picture? These little guys are also called meadow mice, field mice, ground moles and meadow moles -- a confusing array of terms. They are small vegetarians and resemble a field mouse. Their front teeth are chisel-shaped, eyes and furry ears similar to that of a mouse. If you see one, you may think you are looking at a mouse, but if the tail is very short, you will know it is a vole. Their eating habits include a wide variety of vegetation. They feed in lawns and gardens devouring bulbs, roots and whole plants. When food supplies become scarce in winter, orchards suffer much damage, for they will feed on tree barks and girdle main roots of fruit trees, causing enough damage to kill them.

Voles will make their own system of tunnels but do not leave hills of earth like moles. They will also use mole tunnels as runways to get to the plants they enjoy most.

Some damage by voles can be avoided by wrapping valuable tree trunks with 18- or 24-inch high wire mesh, or a commercial nursery tree wrap and establishing a vegetation-free zone around those trees. Eliminating weeds and piles of litter is a good start in reducing vole population. Voles can be caught with mousetraps. Bait the traps with peanut butter or apple pieces. Effective rodent controls and fumigants are available to buy with complete instructions and cautions.

Or you can make your yard a home to a happy cat who is a very good mouser.

Moles and voles -- there's a difference.

Checklist

✔ Before you get involved in any earth-moving landscape project, know where your utility lines and cables are buried. It's easy to forget exactly where they are. Pennsylvania has a system that works. Call toll-free 1-800-242-1776 or access their website: www.paonecall.org.

✔ Watch out for clear, windless nights especially at the time of full moon. That's when frost is most likely to occur.

✔ Cat tails enhance arrangements but can explode into a million fluffy seeds. Spray the heads with hair spray to prevent this. Goldenrod can also be hair-sprayed to prevent "fluffing" in arrangements.

✔ New shrubs and trees need watering throughout the autumn. Even though the weather will turn frosty, it can still be dry. Continue the watering until the ground freezes.

✔ Find a grocery box to collect all the aerosol cans in and bring them in for the winter. Leaving them in an unheated garage or toolshed to freeze affects quality of the contents. It is wasteful of those costly cans.

✔ Bagged or boxed fertilizers that have stored well in a tool shed during the summer should be moved to a dry place. Cardboard and paper bagging deteriorate in dampness and can become unglued as the contents attract moisture.

✔ There are not many more days to use porch or deck furniture. Wipe them down for storage.

✔ Here is some good advice. Apply a heavy layer of manure in the asparagus bed after the ground freezes. It serves as both a winter protection and an early source of nutrients in the spring. Also spread it on areas where early plantings of peas, lettuces and onions will be.

✔ Pick pumpkins and winter squash before heavy frost and store in a cool, dry place. Their skins should have become hardened. Cut them from the vine leaving about 2 inches of stem attached.

✔ Clean up the last of the flowering annuals. Do not allow them to lie where Jack Frost got them. Add them to the compost pile.

✔ Set driveway markers in as snow-removal guides before the ground freezes.

✔ While it is still mild outside, pot up some herbs for indoors. They require a very sunny window. Rosemary is one of the tender perennials that should be brought in for the winter. This also includes geraniums and impatiens. (See *Mere Slips of Plants*, October.)

✔ You hate to see coleus killed by frost. It can be cut and brought into the house for rooting in water, if you do not want to bring in pots. When the roots are substantial enough, they can be potted and kept as colorful reminders of the summer.

✔ Lawn grass almost always needs one more mowing in October. Don't skip the job. Grass that stays quite long overwinter, mats under the weight of snows. It sometimes provides the perfect environment for molds.

✔ Do not stand under an oak tree while acorns are dropping. They hurt when they hit you.

Force a Hyacinth

Buy a hyacinth glass (shaped similarly to an hourglass) at a garden store. Fill it with water and place a hyacinth bulb in the neck of the glass so the bulb is suspended about 1/8 inch above the water. Store in a cool, dark place. In about 6 to 8 weeks, the bulb sprout will be 2 to 3 inches tall. Bring it into a bright room. It will grow quickly and bloom, filling your house with fragrance.

Mere Slips of Plants

Now that your garden is gradually being put to bed for the winter, experiment with cuttings and slips taken from a variety of outdoor favorites.

Many cuttings do well being clipped from a main plant. The cuttings should, ideally, be about 6 to 8 inches long. Strip the leaves from the part of the stem that will be immersed in water. The cuttings can remain in something like colored glass bottles or fancy glass tumblers. Push a few everlastings into each container to make an arrangement. Turn them occasionally to prevent leaning. Several can be clustered on a window sill in adequate light. You will find that they are easier to care for than potted ones.

> *"Sweet potatoes quickly make vines that can...trail around a window or along a shelf."*

Once the cuttings are in water, nature takes over. Little roots start growing on the submerged stems and soon new leaves appear on the tops. There are only a few things you need to do to keep them lively all winter. Change the water every 2 or 3 weeks just to keep things fresh. Drop a few grains of water-soluble fertilizer at each water change.

Many but not all plants perform well in water. Some of the highly successful ones are any of the ivies, coleus, impatiens, crotons, Chinese evergreen, aucuba, wax begonias, scarlet sage, wandering Jew and pussy willow. If the roots develop excessively, there are choices: Prune them, or pot the slips.

Vegetables from the grocery or garden can be fun to grow in one of these "water gardens." Sweet and white potatoes, pineapple tops, carrot and beet tops. Regarding potatoes, choose a half-potato that has at least several eyes. The leaf shoots will come from there. Sweet potatoes quickly make vines that can be interesting to trail around a window or along a shelf. Others can be just an inch or so of the top part of the vegetable and placed to lie in a shallow dish of water or suspended with toothpicks in something like a jelly jar. Soon the tops will sprout leaves to make attractive greenery.

herb of the Month
Barberry

Barberry (*Berberis vulgaris*) is hardly considered an herb, but it may be a plant you should think about for your own garden.

It is a perennial shrub which can grow as tall as 8 feet, but it rarely does so, unless it grows unnoticed in some unoccupied space. There are pretty yellow flowers in the spring and oval seeds that become scarlet red berries in the autumn. The leaves are small like an elongated oval. Unfortunately for anyone who wants to handle it, it is rife with needle-sharp thorns.

Beneath its thin, grey bark is bright yellow inner wood and yellow sap. This, the leaves and roots were all considered medicinal.

If you plan a knot garden , barberry is the shrub to choose. It is easily twisted or pruned to your heart's desire, taking any shape you wish to give it, and being comfortable with it. It is excellent for hedges and topiaries. Make it round, square, pyramidal, make a Mickey Mouse -- it will be happy to oblige.

Dwarf barberry bushes are available, as well as varieties with red or bronze leaves. They stay small and make a very desirable, low hedge at the edge of an ornamental garden with very little maintenance. They are either deciduous or evergreen. If you like the effect of seeing bright red berries, choose the deciduous, for they show off prettily after the foliage drops, staying red all winter.

They grow best in fertile and well-drained soil, in full sun or partial sun and have no strong demands.

Now for the kitchen uses of barberry, which may be surprising. Rich in vitamin C and pectin, the seeds taste like a cranberry with a hint of citrus, and are very tart. Add them in jams, jellies and preserves. They can be substituted for rose hips in recipes. They can be candied to decorate a cake top. Crushed and cooked in a syrup, barberries can be served with pancakes, waffles and as a meat accompaniment.

You may not be interested in using any part of this plant or having it (and its thorns) in your landscape. Alas, it is known to be an invasive and worthy of being pulled up in the wild. But a few cultivated, cared-for plants can add an extra dimension to your gardens.

In a Witch's Garden

Ghouls, goblins and witches are prevail now, seeping out of haunts to hover over places where mortals tread. Watch out. The Jack-o-lantern will light your path but do not stumble into the witch's garden.

What does she grow there? Ah, you had to ask. Well, she grows things of ill repute and strange omen.

We would find hemlock, but not the tree. This would be the herb *Conium maculatum*. Even though this herb is a member of the friendly carrot family, for ages it has been used as a deadly poison. It was the herb of capital punishment in ancient Greece. The Greek philosopher Socrates died after drinking the juice of the plant. We wouldn't want this is *our* garden.

We would probably find foxglove. This is also known as Witch's Thimbles (*Digitalis purpurea*). In proper doses it is used as a heart medication but as all witches know, an overdose is fatal!

We would find monkshood growing. Now, monkshood (*Aconitum napellus*) has been used traditionally to poison spears and arrow heads, and was used by witches, combined with bella donna, to make a flying unguent.

Trees would include ash (*Fraxinus excelsior*). Ash was necessary near this garden, for ash wood is known to be very strong and sinuous. It is necessary for broomsticks. Every witch knows that.

Bloodroot (*Sanguinaria canadensis*) exudes a blood-colored juice from stem and roots. Could it possibly be used as a substitute for "blood of bat" in recipes of black magic?

Love apples (or tomatoes), are related to nightshade, bella donna and other poisonous plants. Prior to the 17th century no one would dare eat the fruit. Perhaps in the witch's garden she grows a nice, black variety (Black Prince, a Russian treasure, or even the Black Brandywine).

Deadly jimson weed (*Datura stramonium*) is probably in the witch's garden, for every part of this plant is poisonous. It is a member of the nightshade family. Do not fall into the jimson weed patch, for it is thorny. Witches call this the thorn apple for good reason.

Ah, and there will be morning glory vines (*Ipomoea purpurea*) growing in wild profusion. Its lengthy vines have been used by witches, folklore tells us, to wrap around a quarry or victim seven times in order to cast a wicked spell. Witches were always careful to use this technique three days before a full moon, or the spell would fail.

We all know that witches do not exist, but once upon a time, long, long ago, there was a woman who did exist who lived in the mountains. Her log hut was in the woods on the edge of town. She was often seen in the woods and meadows in search of herbs with which she practiced herbal medicine for normal, decent folk, who wanted to protect themselves from spells and illnesses. Most all herbs, while applied properly and with discretion, healed and soothed. Perhaps centuries ago, and longer, some of these herbs were used to commit murder and mayhem. History books tell us. There are actually no bad herbs or plants -- only the way in which they are used.

Spathiphyllum

Spathiphyllum has many aliases and is quite a shady character. It is known as white sails, peace lily and spathe flower. It's a friend to many who like easy-care house plants. Its blossoms consist of a large white spathe on the end of a long stem. The white spathe is actually a bract. The flower itself is the small club-like finger held at the base of the white bract.

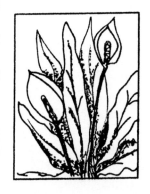

From now until March it needs bright light (but not direct sun). For the rest of the year, it can be situated in a low-light area.

It needs high humidity. If your rooms are dry, place beneath the plant a tray with an inch of pebbles. Keep water in the pebbles, and the plant on top of the pebbles. Water as usual. Fertilizer is not needed until March. From then until autumn, use a house plant fertilizer about once a month.

For the winter, it will rest in its bright spot and you will enjoy its homey cluster of green leaves.

Spring Bulbs

Spring bulbs are a permanent addition to your garden. If your bulb shopping has not been done yet, get busy. Your planting can be done any time until frost occurs or the ground hardens. But why make it uncomfortable for yourself? It's not much fun working in nippy breezes and cold earth, so choose a sunny, mild day this month in which to get bulbs planted.

Someone I know forgot to plant her bulbs last fall. They were found in the spring when she was rattling through the garden tools looking for something else. If this happens to you, they can still be planted in the spring, but only if they haven't already dried out or turned mushy. Some may have already started sprouting. Plant them as soon as possible and let nature take over. You will either be pleasantly surprised by growth, or they will turn to compost in the ground.

Look over the varieties in store displays with an open mind. There is a much wider variety in catalogs, so look at them for flower color, size and blooming time. There are early, mid-season and late-blooming ones. With care, you can plan a very long period of spring flowers. Review them all and then make your informed selections.

Masses of flowers offer much more in the way of impact, than do singles. One idea is to plant your bulbs in "clumps." By that, I mean 3 to 6 of one color in a grouping. Then, clumps can be staggered in your planting area. When clumping bulbs, keep the bulbs somewhat apart from each other in the ground and not shoulder-to-shoulder, for over time, they will expand to form newer bulbs. This is when crowding occurs. The only other thing to keep in mind when planting is to place the taller varieties behind the smaller or shorter ones.

When adding to established beds, it is important to mark where the current bulbs are. Use something like popsickle sticks or tabs cut from a plastic milk jug. Do this before the foliage dies back in mid-summer.

Unfortunately, bulbs are eaten by various kinds of wildlife. Deer will graze on foliage and flowers of all spring bulbs, except daffodils. Both the foliage and the bulbs of daffodils are toxic to animals.

Voles enjoy delicious feasts of bulbs. (See *Moles, Voles, What's the Difference?*, September.) If you know you have a vole problem, take precautions to protect your bulbs by planting them in wire mesh or plastic berry baskets.

If possible, try keeping your spring bulbs out of perennial beds. There are reasons for this. Daffodil foliage can last for 3 or more months before it dries up. Meanwhile, it is in the way of many other plants in the garden. Cutting the foliage back prevents necessary nutrients from getting to the bulbs for next year's flowers. They can be combed together to lie under something nearby. Letting them lie loose looks more natural than if they were knotted or banded together.

In addition, if spring bulbs are planted in a perennial or annual bed, the fertilizing and watering that is needed for the plants may overwhelm the bulbs while they are dormant.

A great place for bulb planting may be under large trees where grass cutting does not take place, or used as accents in a shrub border, or a mulch bed that surrounds a tree planting.

When choosing spring bulbs, don't stop at tulips, crocuses, hyacinths and daffodils. Look at others that give a wider range of blooming time, different textures, and colors. Check catalogs for information on things like grape hyacinth (*Muscari*) in many different colors and types of bloom, snowdrops (*Galanthus*, see *Flowers in the Snow*, February), spring snowflake (*Leucojum vernum*), wood hyacinth (*Scilla*), and Grecian windflower (*Anemone*) in many, very bright colors. Look also, at the checkered lily (*Fritillaria meleagris*) and tall, dramatic *alliums* in many heights and colors. You will be surprised at the number of choices there are, once you start looking.

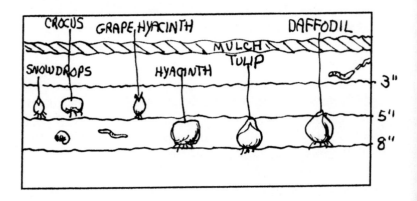

Pest Portraits
Woodchucks

Woodchucks are also known as groundhogs or whistle pigs. There is one that goes by the name of Punxsutawney Phil. He is the popular, four-footed weather prognosticator, who is consulted every February 2nd. In Pennsylvania German dialect, groundhogs are referred to as *Grundsow*.

At first sight, you might mistake the groundhog for a beaver. The bushy tail gives it away. It has a round, brown, furry body, weighing up to 15 lbs. and can often be seen in gardens eating all that good green stuff you are trying to raise. They can be considered cute and fun to watch, except when they are mowing down your garden.

They live underground in burrows, preferring open farmland, woodland or roadsides for their homes. When building, they displace a lot of earth and deposit it near the entrance of their tunnel. It can be comical to see a woodchuck sitting atop the mound as it surveys for danger or attractions.

Their tunnels consist of a main entrance which narrows down to a nesting or sleeping chamber and toilet areas. There may be 2 or 3 exits. They keep a clean house, adding debris to the mound at the entrance.

Groundhogs hibernate from October until March. No wonder Phil is groggy when they prod him from his burrow to forecast the weather.

The problem to gardeners lies mostly in their eating habits, devouring things that you have lovingly planted. To farmers using equipment, their burrow holes are serious hazards for farm machinery.

Damage control can consist of electric fences. An alternative is 3 or 4 foot-high wire mesh fencing installed with the bottom buried. Gas cartridges of carbon monoxide can be ignited and dropped into the entrance hole, but only if the user knows where the exit holes are and can plug them. These can be bought at a farm supply store. Neighbors use metal traps available for purchase or rent from hardware stores. It can be baited with fruit or vegetables pieces. When the animal is trapped it should be transported not less than 10 miles away.

Detailed information on control is available at Penn State Cooperative Extension office, located by county and listed in the back of this book.

Leave It

Remember autumns long ago? We burned fallen leaves in the street at the gutter edge. It could be a fun-type project but was the wrong solution to the problem. It fouled the air we breathed and presented fire hazards.

Welcome to the age of environmental enlightenment. We now treat leaves respectfully and actually put them to work for us.

In neighborhood yards, it is a big job to rake or vacuum fallen leaves every autumn, but many of us enjoy the activity, especially if it means we can exercise with the kids at the same time.

Many communities direct householders to rake leaves into the gutter for mechanical pickup. Others require leaves be bagged. No matter how many leaves or bags one puts out for community pickup, a quantity should be reserved for the compost pile, or for another reserve pile nearby.

Composting is a perfect way to recycle leaves. Its benefits include improvement of garden soil and reduces soil compaction and erosion.

There is a slight problem, though. A heavy layer of dry leaves that is piled on top of the compost pile will probably remain there all winter with no decomposition taking place at all. They need moisture in the interior to start decomposing, but too many of them can throw the balance of the working compost pile out of kilter. Too many "browns" and not enough "greens" isn't a good formula for success.

The leaves you plan to add to the compost pile can be gathered together on the lawn and run over with the mower, shredding them into little pieces that accept and hold moisture better. Every week, until the pile becomes frozen, it should be turned with a fork so that the innermost parts have a chance to get rained on. Continue adding discarded kitchen greens and organic scraps as often as possible through the winter. This time of year, there is very little in the way of grass and garden clippings that contribute to a good balance. Even though the pile may freeze, continue adding kitchen greens, peelings, coffee grounds and all those good things. Occasionally, layer on some of those reserved leaves. When winter is over, regular turning can resume. Its product of rich, black earth can be added to your garden soon

Emergency:
The Frost is on the Garden

When one is unprepared for a heavy harvest of produce, how does one cope with it all when the radio weather report predicts below-freezing temperatures this night? It's especially dicey when the fateful weather report is heard on the 6:00 p.m. news and it's already dark outside, and getting colder. Then, the whole family is employed in gathering vegetables and flowers by flashlight.

How in the world does one cope with this kind of sudden harvest?

Flowers pose no problem. There are enough vases, tumblers or bottles for arrangements in every room.

Peppers, hot or sweet, it doesn't matter, can be sliced into rings, spread on a cookie sheet to freeze until solid, then bagged. That job was easy. They're great with fried onions for steak sandwiches.

Zucchinis can be shredded in a food processor, bagged and frozen in 1- or 2-cup portions to add to cakes and breads later on. Someone I know even adds this ingredient to her home-made vegetable soups. You can also try putting zucchinis in plastic bags and hanging them on neighbors' door knobs tomorrow. It might reduce the supply.

An overabundant supply of apples is usually not a problem at harvest time, for they store well. But when pressed, they can be handled very neatly. Canning applesauce works, but there's more. Peeled, sliced apples, laid out on a cookie sheet in the freezer, then bagged when solid, make wonderful apples for pies, crisps and cobblers. All you have to do is take out just the quantity needed for any recipe.

A friend never cans tomatoes any more -- too much trouble. She peels them using the hot-water blanch, quarters them and pops them into freezer storage bags. They work well to use later in any dish that requires canned tomatoes.

Remember the old saying that if life gives you lemons, make lemonade? Well, if Jack Frost comes by with a heavy hand and you must harvest all the green tomatoes, use them green. They are wonderful fried, as in the Fried Green Tomato recipe in *Tomato TLC*, August.

With a special regard for green tomatoes, the question arises: Is it necessary to pick them all at once, or can we cover the plants to keep them on the vine longer?

Warm days often follow an October frost, but when the day time temperature remains at 55 degrees or lower, field ripening is over.

There are ways to sort green tomatoes.

There is a stage called Immature Green. These are very green and rock solid but can still be used in something like marmalade.

The next stage might be called Mature Green. These are hard and very green but the blossom end may suggest a little yellowing. These are good for frying, cooking into chili or stored for later use. The more yellow present, the better the chances of ripening.

There will be in your hasty harvest, those that are still green but are showing a pink blush at the blossom end. These Pinkies have the best chance of ripening on the kitchen countertop. Just give them a week or two. Don't refrigerate.

Then, there is the last category -- the ones with marks on them, or imperfections, or are very small. You can feel justified in tossing them into the compost pile, or you can think up your own uses. How about golf or baseball practice, juggling, lobbing at squirrels, desk paper weight (if it doesn't leak), target practice. Take your pick.

If your church collects vegetables for the needy, offer some of your supply. Local SAACs (Senior Adult Activity Centers) are happy to receive some of your bounty to share among their members. Also, local food banks might accept your donations. Make a few phone calls and share your garden wealth. Someone will welcome your contribution.

> *In the herb garden, harvest leaves*
> *before the weather gets too cool.*
> *The flavor is best when obtained*
> *before night time temperatures drop*
> *below 50 degrees.*

Tool Storage

Now is your chance. End your frantic springtime rummaging, and store your garden tools in proper places this fall so it is not necessary to play hide-and-seek games in the spring.

It took me several years to get the notion in my head that organization needs to be grappled with outdoors, as well as indoors.

For a very reasonable sum, it is possible to buy at hardware stores a 48-inch metal strip which attaches horizontally to any wall -- namely, the garage or tool shed wall. It is equipped with six, two-pronged, sliding hooks that will accommodate any six tools. The hooks slide easily left and right to hold something wide like a leaf rake or narrow like a fork or hoe.

We received one of these gadgets for a gift and liked it so much, we bought several more. It is such a simple device we wondered why we didn't think of it ourselves. Now we never waste time searching for the right tool, for they are all there when we need them.

When all the tools are hanging neatly in place against the wall, it is simple to notice whether or not they are clean or still muddy. Dried mud left on metal parts starts the rusting process as the mud picks up moisture from weather changes. It is a simple matter to rinse off any soil under the hose when getting ready to hang up the tool.

When spring comes, there will be no more annoying searches through jumbles of tools and handles when looking for a special one. Putting things back where they belong on the rack will be easy and quickly become a good habit.

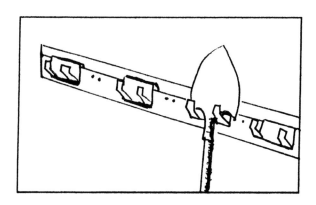

Of Weeds and Wildflowers
Goldenrods

In October, large expanses of goldenrod (*Solidago*) can be seen spreading their joy, dotted with stands of the pink joe-pye weeds and the purple or blue of asters.

For solidago, the main color is gold. There are over 125 species of goldenrod, worldwide; 50 of them are found in the American northeast and New England. Goldenrod stands are the homes to the praying mantis, one of the beneficial insects we like to have in our gardens. Why do the mantids lay their eggs among the goldenrods? Probably because mother mantis spends much of her time there, stalking flying insects that are drawn by the color, scent and nectar of goldenrod plumes.

Early Europeans and American Indians used the goldenrod as a medicinal plant. It was used to settle stomachs and cure wounds. Tuberculosis and bronchitis were also remedied by its application. Nicolas Culpeper, an early herbalist, wrote, "It is a sovereign wound-herb, inferior to none, both for inward and outward use." Colonial women used this native plant as a tea substitute, and it was so popular, it was eventually exported to China.

Thomas Edison, in the years prior to WWII, experimented with goldenrod as a source of rubber in order to reduce our dependency on the imported product. He actually produced synthetic rubber tires, whose color was, not surprisingly, a mustard yellow. He proved that it was technically possible, but, alas, impractically expensive.

As if this lowly-regarded wildflower didn't have enough going for it, it is also known as a dye plant, creating shades of yellow and gold.

Goldenrod has been maligned as a cause of hay-fever. If it weren't for that one myth, goldenrod may once have been our national flower.

All goldenrods are perennials. They transplant easily and are a natural, tall background for shorter plants and flowers in a cottage-type garden. In an arrangement, their cut blossoms stay fresh for many days. As a garden plant, it has very few demands, growing well in unimproved soil.

Hybrid forms are available through catalogs, proving that it can be used successfully in home gardens.

In Praise of Pumpkins

In the New World, pumpkins were found to be growing in abundance, cultivated by the American Indians. A popular American myth is that the Indian Squanto taught the new settlers to plant pumpkins between the corn stalks. The pumpkin plants shaded out the weeds in the cornfield. If true, it seems to have been good advice and a clue that Indians didn't like to weed the vegetable patch, either.

The variety we know today as the Connecticut Field Pumpkin is a modern cultivar similar to the kind that early New Englanders grew.

The hard-shelled neck squashes are the best cooking varieties. The blue-grey Hubbard is a huge, warty, oval squash that has delicious, bright orange flesh. It can be found at farm stands or farmers' markets. Grocery stores display the smaller, striped green and yellow squashes and the spaghetti squash, all of which can be cooked as a dinner vegetable, similar to the acorn type that we all know.

All of these are hard-skinned, winter squashes. They store well and are sweet to the taste. Cut them in half and bake them, cut side down in an inch of water for about an hour. Season with butter, salt and pepper. Sometimes nutmeg can be added to enhance the flavor.

The great orange pumpkins we use for Halloween are usually called face pumpkins because they are not suitable for cooking. After the holiday is over, use your Jack-o-lantern to feed wildlife. Cut it into pieces and place the pieces outside for birds and little four-footed critters to enjoy.

Since painted pumpkins have become so popular, children's hands stay clean and there is less mess to clean up, but painting is certainly as much of a challenge as carving is.

When the winter squashes appear in the stores and they find their way onto the dinner menu, you'll know summer is over.

For cultivation tips, see *Squash -- Summer, Winter, What's the Difference?* in May.

Savory herb Bread

This bread is perfect for the herb grower. It is rich in flavors of rosemary, savory and sage. I've used this bread when I can use my own dried herbs, which always seem more flavorful and fresh-tasting. The recipe makes a 1 ½ lb. loaf in a bread machine. The same ingredients can be used for conventional baking..

3/4 cup flat beer
½ cup water
1/4 cup virgin olive oil
1 tablespoon minced garlic
1 teaspoon crushed rosemary
1 teaspoon ground sage
3/4 teaspoon Kosher salt
½ teaspoon sugar
3 1/4 cups flour
1 3/4 teaspoon bread machine yeast or 2 ½ teaspoons regular dry yeast.

If using a bread machine, add each ingredient in the order given. When adding the yeast, make a hollow in the flour to receive the yeast, keeping it away from the sugar and salt. Use the white bread setting.

When the bread is done but still very warm, spread a light olive oil coating to the top and sides of the loaf with your hands. Before the oil is absorbed, quickly sprinkle with Kosher salt and rosemary leaves. Cool completely and savor.

When using the conventional method, use pans approximately 4x8 inches, greased or sprayed, bake at 350 degrees for approximately 40 to 50 minutes.

November

Checklist

✔ Your glass gazing globe is fragile and while it provided your garden visitors with a fish-eye view of your garden in bloom, it is time to bring it inside for the winter. The fluctuating cold temperatures and heat from sun-load can produce sweat on the inside, damaging the silvering.

✔ Mark the locations of parsnips, horseradish, rhubarb, asparagus and other root crops so you will know exactly where they are when tilling time comes.

✔ Make sure all spray cans and liquids that can be damaged by freezing have been brought in for storage.

✔ If you have been pleased with Brussels sprouts from your garden, the best is yet to come. A good frost has a way of making their flavor even better. Stretch the season by mulching heavily to keep the soil from freezing for just a little while longer.

✔ For those who like a balled, live Christmas tree for the holidays, prepare the hole for it now. You will be thankful you did when the time comes in January to put it out only to discover that the soil has become rock-hard.

✔ Dress up ordinary house plant pots for the winter by putting them in brass pots, glazed pottery crocks or elegant china jardinieres.

✔ You have spent time and energy making your garden soil soft and loose. Help keep it that way by adding a layer of compost for the winter. (See *Till We Meet*, November.)

✔ If you did not bring in the parsley for the winter, it can be kept from freezing by inverting a basket over it that is stuffed with leaves. It provides good insulation. When I do this I sometimes find the field mice have snuggled there for the winter. Lucky for us, they do not eat parsley.

✔ If roses showed signs of black spot, rake the leaves and take them away. The disease overwinters and will spread again next spring if the leaves are not removed.

✔ By now, most of the autumn leaves have been raked up. Don't overlook the raingutters. Leaves pile up in there and we don't even notice. If your gutters have not been fitted with leaf-deflectors, empty them now before the weather brings freezing temperatures.

✔ When discarding purchased corn stalks that were used for autumn decorations, keep them out of the compost pile, even though it seems like a good idea to add them. It's possible they came to your yard with corn borers. It's hard to know, so bag them with the trash.

✔ If keeping some leaves lying around shrubs and on gardens seems the right thing to do for the winter, read on. Leaves become saturated, layered and form a heavy matting, which can actually smother plant roots.

✔ Be an early bird. Decorate with outdoor lights and holiday decorations in November while temperatures may still be mild.

✔ Take time to jot down the last few records in your garden journal. The information may be important to you next growing season.

✔ It doesn't hurt to buy an early supply of road salt or ice melt now before the first storms come. That is when the stores are sold out!

✔ Put your snow shovels in a handy place now, for after the snow flies is not the time to be looking all over for them. If necessary, buy another one or two now before they are sold out.

Aphids can sometimes suddenly appear on potted window sill herbs. When bringing new plants inside, plant a few small, discarded garlic cloves close to the herb in the pot. They will sprout and, I am told, will prevent the aphids from developing. The garlic can also be cut for winter cooking.

Till We Meet

Tilling the soil in your gardens at this time of year has benefits. It may not be necessary to till at all, and I never do. I have raised beds, and I know my son's roto-tiller fits in the beds and works well. The question in some minds may be, "If I've worked hard to improve soil quality and tilth, why would I till it in the fall?"

The answer is that churning the soil exposes hibernating insects and hidden weed seeds, causing them to perish. Perhaps some of them will perish via your feathered friends looking for a meal. The birds, who have worked well for you last growing season, should be in line now waiting for their rewards.

Be careful not to till where there any roots of perennials, for they could be seriously damaged. After tilling, layer on a coating of compost or manure for the winter, and all will be ready for early spring plantings.

Starting Paperwhites

Paperwhite narcissus bulbs are one of the easiest plants one can grow indoors. They don't need a dark, cold-storage, dormant period. They produce fresh, fragrant blossoms in about 6 to 8 weeks, standing in just pebbles or gravel. Soil is an option. They can be started any time from November through late January.

Select a shallow pottery, or plastic dish for your paperwhites. A 10-inch bowl or container can hold up to 8 paperwhite bulbs.

Fill the bowl with moist potting soil, or a bed of pebbles. (I found that pebbles are the most widely accepted medium, but in potting soil, the blossoms seem to last longer.)

Nestle the bulbs, pointy-side up, into the pebbles or soil, about 1/4 inch apart. Apply a little additional pebbles or soil around each bulb until only the tip and shoulders are visible.

Water carefully but thoroughly, keeping soil evenly moist, and with pebbles, keeping the waterline almost up to the bulb bottoms.

Place the planter in a light place where the temperature is cool. Shoots will emerge from the tips. When they reach about 2 or 3 inches tall, the container can be moved to a warmer room in a bright window.

We noticed that if the room temperatures range around 65 to 70, the stems stay a little shorter than those bulbs that were brought into a warmer room. Higher temperatures seem to make the plant grow taller, sometimes toppling over before or during blooming.

Why be satisfied with just one bowl of them, when another container of paper whites can be started every 2 weeks or so?

They are not frost hardy for outdoors, and will not bloom again after being forced once, so should be discarded into the compost pile after blooming.

Batten Down the hatches

October left us with a flurry of Halloween activities and November came in almost unnoticed.

There are almost always things to do outside as we steadfastly "batten down the hatches" for winter. I love the changes in seasons, keeping me busy cleaning up after one to prepare for the next. There is a lot of anticipation in this activity. Each season has its own beauties.

It is best to check on vines that are growing near or on the house. In particular, wisteria and trumpet vines are heavy twiners and can be troublesome without your realizing. If they grow up or very near your shingles and gutters, chances are that shoots have been creeping beneath them, prying them loose. Ivy is guilty of this, and creeping euonymous, as well. They can sometimes get behind shutters. Examination, then pruning, are the best hedges against damage from vines.

Add Color to Winter

A dd more color to gardens by introducing shrubs that are eye-catching all winter long. There are many varieties with interest. One in particular is the winterberry (*Ilex verticillata*). The brilliant red berries brighten the dreariest months of winter. Birds also come to partake, adding movement and even more color to the scene.

Winterberry is a native shrub that bears plum-shaped, green leaves and is a swamp-dweller. Happily, it is not disease prone. It thrives in poor, soggy soil and tolerates shade as well as some sun. However, plants in full sun give the best berry production; less in more shady spots. In its natural habitat it is

> *"...brilliant red berries endure during the dreariest months of the winter."*

most often seen at roadsides or in woods. It is deciduous and grows from six to ten feet tall, bearing numerous red or orange clusters of berries along the stems, always with a black dot at the blossom end. Cuttings of this plant can usually be found in garden shops at Christmas time for indoor arrangements.

Being a true holly, this plant is dioecious, meaning that individual plants are either male or female.

Transplanting of these native shrubs from their natural habitat is not recommended, as too many perish from this act. Instead, take cuttings or use seeds for new plants, bearing in mind that a female cutting will need a male cutting, too.

Purchasing from a nursery is, by far, the most desirable route for immediate gratification. Your nurseryman or home catalog will be able to show or describe dwarf cultivars, as well.

Look also for Red Twig or Golden Twig dogwoods which are deciduous shrubs. In the summer they bear clusters of creamy flowers and in winter, grace the garden with bright red or yellow branches.

Viburnums offer interest and color through most of the year, as well, with their creamy spring flowers, bright autumn foliage and winter berries.

Anyone Into Bonsai?

I visited a greenhouse to discover many Bonsai plants. Asking about them, I learned that the two owners have formed a Bonsai society and teach classes in this ancient art.

To clarify Bonsai, it is originally a Chinese art form that uses horticulture to sculpt three-dimensional forms. The word Bonsai, literally translated, means "tree in a pot." Over the centuries, it has been the Japanese who have perfected it into the form that we know today.

Basically, any plant can be used, but outdoor nursery stock, such as junipers, respond best. Indoor tropicals can be used -- jade, cerissa, weeping ficus and schiflerra. Flowering plants, like wisteria, and crab apple and apple, are used successfully. I was shown a dwarfed Japanese maple that was exquisite. I was told that the leaves of this tree changed colors in the autumn, dropped and would releaf again in the spring.

Specialized tools are not a necessity, but certain ones make a good job better. Commonly used is a concave cutter, wire cutters, tweezers and a pick for pulling apart root balls. A pruning paste used on crown cuts makes a perfect seal with no scars.

Trees that are selected for Bonsai culture should be potted in special, shallow dishes called training pots. These could be of clay or plastic, but stoneware and ceramic are best. They are usually square-shaped, rectangular or oval. The pot should be suited to the size and style of the tree going into it.

When selecting a plant for Bonsai culture, a good deal of attention should be given to its basic form and three-dimensional potential; that is, the trunk or stem and the situation of its branches. A form should already be in the gardener's mind as to what special style he will want this plant to assume -- low horizontal, literati, clouds, cascade. Then the pruning starts. I was told it almost hurts to brutally cut and snip branches and roots until one grows accustomed to the process and sees wonderful results taking shape.

The key to Bonsai, then, is repeated pruning of a selected plant to achieve miniaturization and the ultimate desired shape. Some of a person's soul goes into Bonsai culture, for each one is a living, miniature treasure.

Gardenias

Everyone loves those exquisite plants with glossy, green leaves, creamy white blossoms that impart a heady fragrance. One blossom can perfume a whole room.

In the store, their multiple buds offer promise of bloom and tempt us to buy. We envision every bud in bloom -- well, almost every one -- we would settle for a few unopened ones dropping off.

How many times have we brought home a gardenia plant full of promise, only to be disappointed?

They are very temperamental, but so would you be if you were snatched away from your warm, humid home and forced to stand around in cool rooms with wet feet.

There are two kinds of gardenias. One is the winter-blooming, *Gardenia veitchi* and is difficult even under ideal greenhouse conditions. No wonder we have had so many failures.

The other one is the *Gardenia florida*, a summer-blooming variety, blooming easily while being kept outdoors and having a winter resting period. Its flower is smaller than the *veitchi*, but just as fragrant.

If you already have this kind, I can offer some hints. It requires indoor temperatures about 70 degrees daytime, and no less than 60 degrees at night time. Leaves will turn yellow and drop if night temperatures fall below 60 degrees and the buds will fail if that night temperature is too close to 70. New buds will not set if temperatures are above 60. It sounds complicated.

It also requires bright, eastern sun in the morning and about 4 hours of it, if that's possible. Cantankerous? Yes.

To provide necessary humidity, fill its saucer with pebbles or sand and water. Keep it filled with water to just below the surface and not touching the pot. Lightly misting the foliage several times a day is an alternative.

Good luck with your temperamental beauty. You are equal to the challenge.

Don't Guess:
Do a Soil Test

Soil testing is a valuable source of information for the home gardener. It checks for soil pH (see *Soil pH,* May), and existing nutrients, and makes recommendations for the proper fertilizer for your particular growing circumstances. Tests may be done any time of year -- even in November. If you found that things you planted last season didn't live up to expectations, perhaps the soil was out of balance for them. Now you can find out by using a soil test kit.

Proper soil fertility is an important ingredient in all plant health, from turfgrass, to shrubs, trees, all annuals and perennials. Guessing about nutritional needs is pointless.

"A soil test kit is not an expensive investment to help your garden do its best..."

Soil test kits are available at any Penn State Extension Office for a small price. For an analysis of several sites on your property, a test kit may be bought for each site. Penn State offices, addresses and phone numbers are listed in the back of this book for each county. Contact yours to find out how to get a kit for your garden.

The procedure is simple, and is explained fully with each test kit. Basically, gather soil samples from several areas within your garden, collecting them in a clean bucket or clean paper bag. Take samples of soil from several inches deep, discarding things like stones or sod. Enclose the sample in the pouch for mailing.

A questionnaire comes with each kit, asking you to indicate what is or will be growing in the tested area and asks a few other questions about your garden.

After mailing, results should come back to you in about 2 weeks. If there are any questions in your mind about interpreting the information sent you, your county agent will be glad to explain.

A soil test kit is not an expensive investment to help your garden do its best.

What is IPM?
Integrated Pest Management

Usually, when we see an insect on one of our plants, most of us go into a mild panic, imagining that the whole garden is under attack. This panic takes us to the store for a handy pesticide which eliminates the pest -- quickly, surely, and extremely.

We have a lot to learn about natural processes of nature. In learning these processes, we find that there is a delicate balance between insects and their predators. This knowledge brings us to understand that there is another approach to the pest problem. It is known as IPM (Integrated Pest Management). IPM manages the health of plants with minimal pesticide use.

Only three to five percent of all insects are harmful, and more importantly, most pests have natural enemies such as frogs, toads, beneficial insects and birds to keep their numbers controlled.

The IPM method tries to avoid problems. All plants have a natural defense system that is used against pests. These defenses work well when the plant is not under stress. Stress can be caused by many things: too dry conditions, too wet conditions, wrong soil type, too hot, too cool, not enough sunlight or too much. Stress can be avoided by choosing them wisely and planting carefully. There are steps we can take that will produce healthy gardens and landscapes.

Choose plants wisely that are suited to your area. If, for instance, your soil is acidic, use ones that prefer acid conditions. Choosing full-sun plants for a shady garden would be a poor choice. Also, think about using plants that are native to your area.

Plant carefully. Help them get a good start by following instructions from the nurseryman, or from the plant tabs that come with seedlings. Learn the do's and don't's for applying mulch. (See *Removing the Mystery of Mulch,* April.) Used correctly, it is a valuable tool.

Boost plant health. This is done by providing the best growing conditions. Get the soil tested (see *Don't Guess; Use a Soil Test,* November.) and follow the test recommendation, preparing the soil properly before planting and using fertilizers only when needed. We are sometimes inclined to over-fertilize. Keep new plants watered regularly until established.

Keep plants groomed. Debris builds up in gardens and collects at the base of some plants. Rake it away. Remove dead portions of plants, and leaves and branches that have fallen. If a branch is broken or diseased, remove it. Again, apply mulches properly, making sure no mulch touches the main stem or trunk of your plants. All these suggestions will produce vigorous plants that are less susceptible to disease and insects.

Take that "estate inspection" tour frequently and regularly to monitor what is going on. You will be alert to any unusual changes that are taking place. If a pest does show up, natural enemies may be around to prey on it. You may have to learn some tolerance to some plant injury before the harmful insect has become controlled by the beneficials.

It may be helpful to buy a garden insect identification book. Spend time at the book store browsing, until you find a book that will be useful. I have several such books and use them often. You may identify a beneficial. If so, what is it preying on? This is all good stuff you will want to know. Pests are naturally a part of the environment, and trying to eradicate as many as you see is unrealistic. The focus on IPM is to keep plants healthy and monitor conditions. If treatment of some sort is needed, then physical controls (hand-picking of bagworms, rinsing aphids off with water spray, traps, removing infected plant part) or biological controls (introducing beneficials into the area, use of Bt -- *Bacillus thuringiensis*) are strongly suggested. Chemical controls include environmentally safe ones such as horticultural oil and insecticidal soap.

The last resort should be conventional pesticides. They are toxic to our environment, affecting both us and all wildlife. Used judiciously, they can manage the extreme problem.

> Remember that when you use a pesticide to kill the "bad" bugs, you may also be killing the "good" bugs.

Of Weeds and Wildflowers

Valerian

The dried roots of valerian (*Valeriana officinalis*) have been used as a sedative and relaxant since early times; in fact, was even included in field doctors' medical kits on Civil War battlefields.

Native to Europe and Asia, it grows wild in moist, wet environments, and is today cultivated in many European countries for medicinal use. It is available in our health food stores and in pharmacies.

As a garden plant, It is an old-time favorite. It is also known by the name garden heliotrope.

It is grown as a 3- to 5-foot tall, hardy, background perennial that provides very pretty, loosely clustered pink to pale mauve blossoms at the top of tall stalks from June through late summer. The blossoms have an exceedingly sweet fragrance, but the root, from which medical formulas are made, smell rather putrid. "Like dirty gym socks," says one grower, or "like the odor of an aged cheese," says another. Another grower who stores dried roots in a tightly sealed Mason jar, claims it still smells up the closet where it is stored.

It is not a fussy plant, tolerating full sun as well as some shade and a wide range of pH. It does need moist, soil that contains lots of organic matter.

Seeds are obtained through catalogs as an herb. But once established in your garden, it will reseed itself freely. It is a great conversation piece and visitors will love its fragrant flowers.

Sleepy Time for Mother Nature

Anyone who is a gardener is inherently tuned in to the changes of seasons. While driving along country roads in the autumn, it may be common to see box turtles crossing the road, probably trying to get to a good place to burrow for the winter. Most people will stop and lift the turtle, putting it in the grass in the direction it was going. By now the chipmunks have disappeared and so have many birds and insects.

But where do they go when the days become shorter and temperatures drop? Turtles, like insects, snakes and frogs are cold blooded, meaning that their body temperatures rise and fall with surrounding temperatures. In fact, it is easy to believe that these cold-blooded creatures are better suited to a long period of cold better than we are. Our own efforts of maintaining a constant body temperature has brought us to employ elaborate tricks to keep ourselves appropriately warm or cool.

> "At the first hint of lowering temperatures, insects become inactive and go into a suspended animation."

At the first hint of lowering temperatures, insects become inactive and go into a suspended animation. During this time, they do not, or cannot, eat, grow, reproduce or even move. This dormancy period is how they have adapted throughout time to increase their chances of survival.

How about butterflies? Their life cycle includes four stages: egg, caterpillar, chrysalis and adult. In most species, nature has provided for them rather meagerly, choosing only one of these stages in which they can safely overwinter. This wintering stage can be different from specie to specie, but here are some examples.

Swallowtails overwinter in the form of a chrysalis, firmly attached to plants or foliage where the hatched caterpillar will feed in the spring. The same is true of the spicebush butterfly that uses the twigs of the spicebush to lay eggs where their caterpillars will enjoy early spring meals from the emerging leaves and blossoms of the spice bush. Viceroy, white cabbageworm and orange sulfurs also spend the winter as a chrysalis. In some cases, some adults of these can outlast a winter in their adult stage.

The monarch is a special case. It actually migrates to Mexico to spend the winter and returns unfailingly each spring.

Why don't the overwintering ones freeze to death? They use tricks that they have instinctively evolved. One is in their behavior of hiding. In the summer, you know how many insects can be seen in fields or woods. They certainly are active and moving around. But in preparation for their dormancy, many go into hiding in such places as under pieces of leaf litter, rocks, pieces of peeling bark or other debris. Others can dig their way into several inches of soil.

Their body chemistry helps, as well, causing them to reduce the freezable water content of their bodies and produce glycerol that lowers their body fluids' freezing point. So they winterize their bodies much as we winterize our cars.

Butterfly boxes have become popular garden decorations, but, hating to destroy your fun, research has shown that butterflies really don't care. The boxes end up as shelters for spiders, mice or wasps. That's fine, though. The pretty, painted boxes look great in a butterfly-friendly garden and are very pretty attention-getters. Enjoy yours if you have any, but after millions of years of evolving, butterflies find adequate hiding places to overwinter on their own.

More hibernation Tricks

Gardeners battle rabbits, raccoons, woodchucks and moles all summer, and in the autumn, put their gardens to bed for the winter. Then, where do these pesty animals go? Some go to bed, too (hibernate) and emerge after a winter's sleep with big appetites at the same time we are waiting for our seeds to sprout.

Woodchucks (or groundhogs) are true hibernators. They burrow down several feet into a pile of firewood, under a porch or shed. They make tunnels that run up to 50 feet in length with openings on each end. By Thanksgiving, the days are sufficiently cool that they curl up and go to sleep in the tunnel where their respiratory systems and metabolisms drop to a point close to death. Even though February 2nd is Groundhog Day for us, they don't usually waken until much later in the month or in March.

Moles do not hibernate. They just stay underground tunneling through the soil all winter, keeping very busy. They are often blamed for "disappearing" tulip bulbs and damaged plants. In fact, they eat the grubs that they find underground. So we should blame the bulb-eating on field mice who also use the mole tunnels. During a mild winter, the mole tunnels will be close to the surface. As weather worsens, their runs go deeper.

Rabbits do not hibernate, either. They tough it out, sheltering under backyard sheds, RV campers or in thickets of evergreens. When snow covers the grass that they eat, then it is off to the young trees for some tasty bark.

Raccoons live similarly, but have the added advantage of being able to de-lid a garbage can and chew through plastic containers of pet feed. Their front paws are just like hands and are as useful as our own. Raccoons just mark time all winter until it is time to raid the garden patch in the spring.

Chipmunks that frolic in the landscape are ever so cute. I supply cracked corn during the summer. They fill up their cheeks to take to their dens in the rock walls. A caution -- do not to make pets of these little visitors. If they should take up residence under the porch, a large-enough colony of them can undermine foundations. The same is true of woodchucks. They will disappear from your landscape during October. Chipmunks make snug dens in which to hibernate.

A Cactus Dish Garden

Take a look at cactus plants in a greenhouse. They are quite bizarre with strange contours, vastly-varied textures and vivid blossoms. After all, they have learned to exist by adapting in the harshest of conditions.

Single specimens are fun to care for as a hobby and to exhibit as such. Dish gardens of cacti can be equally interesting. Their dishes or pots can be any ceramic dish, bulb pan or Bonsai pot. One requirement is that there be some sort of drainage hole in the bottom.

Soil for our cacti will be a special cactus mix (worth buying) or equal parts potting soil and sand. In lieu of sand, perlite can be used.

The main expense will be the plants. Follow the old oriental rule of using an odd number, such as 5, 7 or 9. The number, of course, would depend on size of container. In choosing plants, vary the textures, form and height.

Gather all your materials and you're ready to start. Arrangement of plants depends on whether your dish garden will be viewed from all sides or only one. All sides: tallest go in the center surrounded by shortest ones. For one-side viewing, the tallest go in the back; shortest in front. Put trailing ones near the edge so they can flow over the pot.

When transferring plants into their new container, the stickery ones can be grasped by a strip of paper. Break up the root ball. Tamp the soil lightly around each plant and apply a half-inch of some sort of top dressing. This would be aquarium pebbles in colors or natural, or crushed oyster shells (chicken grit sold at feed stores) or crushed stones. This is not just a cosmetic application; it aids in air circulation and holds the plants firmly. Landscaping can be added for fun, like a small toy dinosaur or lizard. It's *your* garden, so you may get creative.

Do not water this garden for at least a week. Roots need this time to adjust. After that, water lightly, letting the soil dry out between waterings. Keep the garden in full sun.

Remember that this garden is not a permanent thing. In time the plants will outgrow their space. When it becomes lopsided or shaggy, it is time to repot, dividing or snipping off shoots for a new garden. Then add a few new cacti and create a new design.

194

Witch hazels

Witch hazels (*Hamamelis virginiana*) are very hardy, small, ornamental trees that reach a mature height of about 15 feet. When most other trees have lost their leaves in the autumn, witch hazels burst forth in bloom with curious, fragrant blossoms whose petals resemble thin, yellow, twisty straps. Blooming period can last a month or two. When the small fuzzy fruits ripen, about the same time flowers appear, they eject their seeds in small, snapping explosions, shooting 15 feet or more; hence, the common name of snapping hazel.

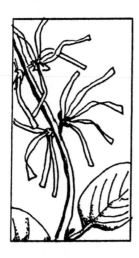

It is a native American plant and is the source of one of our most common home remedies. Bark, twigs and leaves are used in a distillation process that produces witch hazel solution. American Indians taught settlers the uses of this small tree, which was the source of liniments and astringents.

The European species of witch hazel were cut and used as divining rods. The name witch doesn't refer to magic or anything occult, but from the Anglo-Saxon word that means, "to bend."

Woodland is its more amenable home, but will grow in lawns that are overshadowed by tall trees. Planted in a lot of humus or peat moss in moist soil under tall trees, it will make itself very much at home.

It is fascinating to see this tree change with seasons. Summer brings its green leaves and its sheltering form of low branches to make a perfect hideaway to read on a hot day. Autumn changes its leaves to yellow, then as the world turns cold, its strange blossoms appear. A setting of evergreens will enhance the color of its autumn blossoms.

There are many other types of witch hazels available at large nurseries, all of them of approximately of the same stature. Some have red blossoms. Some have autumn foliage which turns orange or red. Branches may be cut during winter and brought indoors to enjoy.

December

Checklist

✔ Are the deer pruning your azaleas and rhododendrons ? Try this Hot Sauce formula: 3 tablespoons of Tabasco sauce, 10 tablespoons Wiltproof, one gallon of water. Spray every ten days, or after rain or snow rinse the formula off. Also apply Ro-Pel on the ground. Both of these can be used year 'round to give plants protection from nibbling wildlife. (See *Oh, Deer*, June.)

✔ Keep watering all your newly-planted shrubs and trees until the ground freezes. This will include those that were planted in the spring.

✔ Red, pink and every other color of poinsettias have appeared in stores now. When buying, be sure you will know how to care for them. Read *Caring for your Gift Plants*, January.

✔ When transporting fresh flowers or plants from the florist or greenhouse at this time of year, be especially careful that they will be wrapped so that blossoms are completely covered with paper or film. Just a minute or two in freezing temperatures can damage tender floral tissues. Put them in a heated car to take home, and don't leave them parked for an hour or two while shopping elsewhere.

✔ With many businesses giving away free calendars to customers at year-end, get one that you will make garden notes in for the coming year. Perhaps you will receive a pretty journal book as a gift. In that case, ditch the calendar idea.

✔ Inventory last summer's seeds. Enter the list in your journal. You will need this information when shopping through catalogs, and if you think, "That's OK; I'll remember what's there," the fact is, it's very easy to forget.

✔ Suddenly your house is overflowing with houseplants that have been brought in from the outside. Some need a dormancy period and should not be fertilized until mid or late winter. Meanwhile, don't neglect them. They have a tendency to dry out quickly in heated rooms. Mealy bugs and other pests can gain a foothold before you know it. (See *Insect Insights: Mealybugs and White Flies,* March.)

✔ Window boxes can look forlorn in the winter. Insert branches of evergreens, holly or pyracantha cuttings. Add a string of white lights to give them a sparkle.

✔ Shrubs that become snow covered are better insulated against sub-freezing weather than those that are not. Plan ahead and tape, or use twine around things such as arborvitae to prevent snow overload and possible breaking. When snow does build up, melt partially, then refreeze, it is especially bad news. Gently tap the snow off the branches with a broom handle, starting at the tips and working back. Just removing some of the snow will greatly reduce the overload.

✔ Salt-based products for ice/snow removal may be used safely if the salt runs off without soaking into lawns or plants. Do not use salt if the temperatures plunge to 20 degrees or lower, for at that number, salt is no longer effective as a melter.

✔ Make little calico bags with ribbon ties filled with seeds from your garden for any gardener on your gift list. (See *Gifts for the Gardener,* December.)

✔ If you notice your indoor geraniums are getting very leggy, it is probably due to lack of sufficient sunlight. Cut them back by about half and try to find a brighter spot for them.

Plant some ground cover in the soil of your largest, tall-stemmed houseplants instead of using Spanish moss. Plant ajuga, baby tears, rock cress, small-leaved ivies, most of which do not require full sun.

Deck the halls
Cuttings for Decorations

Y ou may be surprised to learn that decorating with holly is a tradition that spans many centuries. Few other plants remind us of winter as much as this one does. Cutting branches at this time of year not only beautifies the house for the holiday season, but also serves a purpose of pruning and keeping the tree or shrub in shape.

About pruning, hollies actually need very little of it, once established. Pruning helps retain the conical shape of the shrub and produces thicker growth for next year. The best time for this is December or late winter. Cut the branches just above a bud at a 45-degree angle.

Bring the cut branches in and place the stems in a bucket of water to which a spoonful of sugar has been added. Once arranged, they should be kept in water and be re-watered as necessary.

The other good thing about growing hollies is that they add value to your property, besides providing winter food for birds.

When company comes, it is fun to decorate trays or plates of food with a sprig of seasonal holly, mistletoe or Jerusalem cherry or the deep green of yew cuttings that have plump red berries. Think twice before you do this. Many of these beautiful, seasonal plants should not be used on or near food, for they are not meant to be eaten, and some are actually poisonous. If you really need a touch of green, try wedges or slices of lime, a cluster of grapes, or glossy green gardenia leaves from a florist. Wash before using. The leaves are not meant to be eaten, either, but at least they are not toxic.

Keeping the Christmas Tree Fresh

K eeping your natural Christmas tree fresh should be high on your agenda. The formula for this is an old one, and contains nearly every element that a tree would receive if it were still growing in the ground and drawing up nutrients.

As soon as the fresh tree is brought home, cut the bottom two or three inches off the trunk and make a solution of the following: In a 2-gallon bucket, mix about 10 pints of warm water with 1 pint of white Karo syrup, 2 ounces chlorine bleach, ½ teaspoon borax and 2 pinches of Epsom salts. Keep the tree standing in this solution until it has been brought indoors. Water the tree every day with this mixture for the time it is inside. Turn off the tree lights if you are not in the room.

Your Garden in Winter

The Thanksgiving turkey has been reduced to hash and soup. House plants are settled in now, snoozing while the winter sun arcs low in the sky.

Outside, the bright autumn leaves are no more. Some still lie in places where wind has sent them, crisp and brown, leaving only shades of grey and black among tree branches. At times, winter can be a little dismal, much like the end of something; something you miss. However, even though bright leaves have dropped from branches, close inspection discloses next year's buds, plump and healthy, waiting there for spring's warmth to bring them to life.

A trip to the garden beds bring on certain small emotions. First, the reason for the trip outside was to cut Brussels sprouts, sweetened by the frost. But all around, the garden sleeps. There is no other reason for you to be out there, really, than the sprouts for the table. No self-respecting earthworm would raise its head in these cold temperatures. They are snuggled into the soil waiting for the warmth of spring. The humus, too, settles down and snoozes inertly, while sharing its nutrients with the welcoming soil. And the mice and raccoons? They are off somewhere having a bedtime snack, making themselves fat for the winter. Could you do a little more work outside while looking around? Sure, not all of it was finished yet. If the work isn't finished by the first of December, then it usually won't get done. There is always more that can be tended to, but who's looking? Certainly not us. No, let's amble back to the house with the cold, fresh sprouts. All those uncompleted garden chores can wait now until winter and snow go away. In any case, several new seed catalogs came that we haven't looked at yet. Winter can make the garden sleep, but not the gardener in us.

herb of the Month
Rosemary

Rosemary is the herb of Christmas, signifying it is the time of year to remember loved ones. As a gift it has always been given in remembrance, friendship and love.

This Mediterranean herb is thought to have been used with thyme and bedstraw for Christ's bedding in the manger. It is also said that the Holy Family took refuge in large rosemary shrubs while fleeing the Holy Land, and that its flowers, originally white, turned to blue when Mary hung her wrap on a rosemary bush. Scholars, take note, for in ancient Greece, students wore garlands of it while studying and taking exams, believing that it helped improve memory. More recent uses of this herb was in the war years of the 1940s, when a mixture of its leaves plus juniper berries were burned in hospitals as a germicide. Modern research tells us that rosemary oil does have antibacterial effects.

Leaves gathered in the summer are dried, then used in cosmetic preparations or cooking. Try a rosemary bath to soothe a tired body. For this, make a strong tea from leaves steeped 10 minutes in boiling water and add it to the bath water. After soaking for 20 minutes, you will emerge feeling very much better.

Rosemary has many uses in the kitchen. The one I like best is adding it to a loaf of home-made bread, then dipping the bread in olive oil instead of spreading with butter.

A savory rosemary butter can be made by mixing 6 tablespoons of softened butter with 2 teaspoons of fresh, finely chopped herb. If the herb is dried, use only 1 teaspoon of it in the butter.

In the garden, it is a tender perennial, meaning it must be brought in for the winter in Zone 6. Outdoors, sink pots of it into the garden bed up to the rim. Water it regularly, along with other plants, being careful to keep the soil consistently moist. Fertilize with an all-purpose mix in the spring and again in the fall. When brought indoors for the winter, it needs any place that is cool. Best results are obtained in a sunny room, vestibule or hallway where temperatures stay about 50 to 55 degrees.

This one is not a kitchen windowsill herb, but can be enjoyed to the fullest 12 months of the year.

Of Weeds and Wildflowers
Christmas Fern

When winter comes, there is very little green left for the eye to see, except in the lacy evergreens, rhododendrons and laurels. It is surprising, in looking closer to the ground, to see evergreens of a different kind. They are the Christmas ferns (*Polystichum acrostichoides*).

They are common in Pennsylvania woods and are found by the dozens on shaded slopes and, stream sides. They are also found by old stone walls that their spores have been blown against. They are identified by the bristly leaf tips and the "ear" where the leaflet of the frond meets the stem. Each leaflet resembles a little, green, Christmas stocking.

The Ice Age is credited with bearing this fern from the far north, being found from Canada to northern Florida, and west to Texas and Wisconsin.

This fern was used by American Indians as a medicinal plant. Almost every plant on the planet has some sort of medicinal properties, and the Christmas fern is no exception. The roots made a tea for treatment of

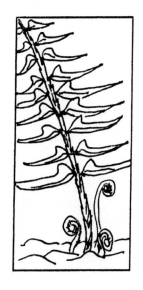

chills, stomach aches, fevers, pneumonia and a poultice was used for rheumatism.

The Christmas fern is wonderful used in naturalizing gardens, along walkways, mixed with spring bulbs and used with shade-tolerant summer flowers. Its foliage accents the beauty of rocks and boulders in rock gardens and adds a softening background by water gardens. Three or four stems can be picked any season of the year to enhance floral arrangements.

In the spring when the new curls of fronds are emerging, some of last summer's fronds may have become ragged and weather-beaten. They can be cut off, or left to compost under the shade of newly maturing fronds.

Gifts for the Gardener

Decentber is the giftiest month of the year and often times, we are hard pressed to know, or even guess, what to give some members of the family. Here is a bonanza of ideas.

Decorative flower pots are available in hundreds of sizes and styles. It may be hard to make a decision on size, so why not buy it and present it with a plant already in it...such as an orchid, or something else less ordinary. Pot prices vary widely.

Pot feet. Pot feet usually come in red clay in ornamental designs. A set of 3 or 4 suspend the pot a few inches off the ground or deck. Their designs are often things like lion's claws, hedgehogs, classic scrolls, or more whimsical frogs. Prices vary, but usually start near $10 and up.

Gazing globes are intriguing and add a special Victorian attractiveness to any garden. They come with or without a pedestal. The simplest pedestal would be a clay birdbath stand, but there are very exotic, inspiring and ornamental ones of wide variety to go harmoniously with the glass globe. Prices can start at $50.

Sundials are truly interesting to examine, for they come small, large or fancy, but all are functional. Mostly, they are of metal construction, some polished brass, some antiqued, some with frogs or hummingbirds, take your pick. They start in price about $30 and go up.

Statuary and hooks are hot items. The trend in gardening is not necessarily the flowers that grow, but how we accessorize them with bunnies, ducks, angels, gargoyles, charming children. All are designed to amuse and fascinate. Choices are endless and such fun to view. Garden hooks are tall, wrought iron posts that support a hanging planter, a basket, a hanging birdbath or feeder. These are priced from about $15.

Signs that instruct, announce or amuse are made of many materials. Slate on leather thongs for hanging, wooden ones on stakes, engraved stones announcing, "Grandmom's Garden," "Turtle Crossing," "This garden is for the birds," and so on. Many are painted with angels or other garden themes. Prices $15 and up.

Gardening books are available on a wide variety of special subjects, or just general, all-purpose gardening, all of which are very helpful for either the occasional or intense gardener. For the woodworker give a book of patterns and directions for birdhouses, garden furniture, storage boxes, garden towers (for climbing vines), pergolas and more. (Price range $15 to $35.)

Faucet handles come in a variety of designs, such as hummingbird, quail, duck, rose and others. They make a classy, attractive substitute for the functional (but not much fun) outdoor faucet handle. This is an especially nice gift in brass or bronze. Prices start about $30.

Gift baskets can contain colorful garden gloves nestled in with new hand tools -- your choice -- a bar of gardener's hand soap, hand lotion, and a small pot of paperwhite narcissus bulbs. Prices vary according to contents.

pH meter offers a quick and easy way to test the acid/alkaline balance of soil. A probe at the end of a meter, inserted into the soil, gives a quick analysis. Another type of soil test kit is one that uses tablets (pills) and color-coded charts to get the analysis a gardener needs. Even better than that, buy a couple of Soil Test Kits offered for about $6.00 each from a County Extension Office. Locations and phone numbers are listed in the back of this book.

Ergonomic rake or snow shovel is an excellent gift choice for anyone. The shank of the tool is bent in 2 strategic places and in such a way as to allow less strain on the user's back -- a boon to all those folks who once in a while complain of back pain.

Imitation owl or falcon make good scarecrows. Made of plastic, they are mounted on posts. They are known to frighten bunnies, birds, mice and woodchucks away. Fake black snakes are also available for the same purpose. However, all of these should be relocated or turned in the garden frequently because visiting nibblers can become accustomed to the ruse and ignore it. Various prices, usually not over $25.

There is much more for gift-giving to gardeners. Look at sturdy hand tools, a garden cart, soil thermometer, rain gauge, a pretty garden journal, or a fancy sprinkling can. If *all* else fails, buy a gift certificate which allows the recipient the fun of shopping and making the choices.

Colorful Cyclamens

Among the plants of the holiday season, cyclamens are pretty much the prima donna. Breeders have been developing this plant in brighter and wider ranges of color, plus adding a bit more perfume to its character.

This plant goes through a blooming period that can last for months. Even when it finishes its blooming period, its mound of thick leaves with silver markings and veins make it an attractive foliage plant. Some varieties sport deep green leaves with yellow-green markings. Flower colors range through the reds, salmons, pinks, fuchsias, lilacs and sparkling white. Display your cyclamen in any kind of pottery or china bowl, or use a soup tureen or a basket.

Keep in a cool room with a nighttime average temperature of about 50 to 60 degrees. Water it in the sink in a pan for about 10 minutes and let water be absorbed from the bottom. Their leaves do not like to be wet. If the soil becomes too dry, leaves can turn brown. If left to become too moist or soggy, the corm can start to rot.

As the flowers fade, the blossom stems can be tugged out, straight up. Left-over stems usually start to rot. You will see more new blossoms forming down in the crown of the plant.

When it is finished blooming, try keeping your cyclamen. It's worth another go-around. During the summer, the leaves will yellow. At this point, allow the soil to go dry. Keep it outside in a dry, shady place (under an overhang), or in a cool basement, keeping the plant barely moist.

In the autumn, look for signs of new growth, repot it with fresh soil and return the plant, in its same pot, to a light area, still keeping barely moist, until a new mound of leaves has formed. From that time on, increase its watering, fertilize, and you should expect blossoms.

If the experiment with rejuvenation is not quite your thing, they are not expensive to buy. One of a large size would be a perfect specimen to display by itself, or a cluster of 5-inch high miniatures is striking in an assortment of colors in a basket or terra cotta bowl. A grouping of 8-inch miniatures of red, fuchsia and white make an interesting and welcome holiday gift.

A Gift of Myrrh

Biblical plants are often ones with which we are familiar. Interestingly, the Holy Lands that border the shore of the Mediterranean, encompass Palestine, Lebanon, Jordan and Syria, are known as "the fertile crescent." Within this area the climate ranges from sub-tropic to sub-arctic -- a very wide range of climate conditions which supports most of the known plants of the world

To name a few, we find almonds, apples, cedars, chestnuts, many herbs that we grow in our own gardens, gourds, garlic and onions, lilies, melons, roses, willows, oaks, beans, figs, flax, and myrrh.

Myrrh (*commiphora myrrha*). It is a small tree or shrub which exudes its sap or resin. We do not know much about myrrh, for it is one that does not grow in this country at all. In the Bible, a reference to it is found in Proverbs 7:17, "I have perfumed my bed with myrrh." And, of course, it is believed to have been one of the 3 gifts that were offered to the infant Jesus by the Magi. It is one of the most ancient medicines and was widely used by Egyptians as a remedy for mouth and throat problems. It was an embalming fluid and was a cure for many of the known diseases of the time which included leprosy.

The substance comes from a small, deciduous tree or large shrub, that bears flowers of yellow-red. Its gnarled branches support twigs that terminate in small, sharp spines. The bark yields a thick, yellow resinous sap that weeps from small fissures or injuries. The sap hardens into crystals, changing color to a semi-transparent, red-yellow or red-brown which has a powdery surface. The tree grows in very hot, dry regions of the Middle East where it thrives in the igneous-formed soil.

In my father's pharmacy of the early 20th century, one of his apothecary jars was marked Myrrh. He used the small, hard gems to make tinctures and powers for skin disorders and throat ailments.

Unfortunately, we are unable to grow or nurture this ancient tree in our own gardens, but many have had questions regarding the source of mysterious myrrh. Many plants of the world have been put here for man to use, and as long as we live here, are free to use them for sustenance -- clothing, shelter and healing -- and should be mindful of the fact that they are only loaned for our use.

A Nutty Subject

According to a survey by U.S.News & World Reports, Americans eat nearly 40 percent of their yearly consumption of nuts in December and January. Today, we open a can or jar of nuts and pour them into a dish, but in days gone-by, it was a "togetherness" activity to sit around the table and eat nuts as the shells were cracked open.

In the northeastern United States there is abundance of black walnuts, hickories, hazelnuts (filberts), and chestnut trees, the crops of which can be used just as fruit crops are. Nut trees are a welcome addition to any back yard, with the possible exception of black walnuts. Black walnuts should be left to the wilds of nature, for the chemical that is found in this variety is toxic to many growing plants that may be nearby.

Nut trees take time to mature, so if you want to include any in your yard, get them growing early in your planning stage. They are valuable trees, not only for their edible fruits but for their natural beauty and shade.

A word of advice to nut tree owners is that if wildlife is plentiful where you live, and hungry enough, they will beat you to your harvest. Therefore, as soon as the nuts start dropping, beat the critters to the punch by picking up the nuts from the ground at least once a day. You probably won't have bushelsful, but certainly, more than enough to please yourself and your friends.

Spring is the best time for planting nut trees so they will have all summer to establish a good root system. Autumn-planted trees may have a higher failure rate because their root structure did not have time to mature before the ground froze. Until the ground freezes, watering should take place on a regular basis.

Filberts do not come from trees, but shrubs. The native American hazelnut (*Corylus americana*) will bear small fruits, but the European filbert (*C. avelana*) bears more practical and better-sized nuts. Most filberts will produce after 3 years. They look attractive as a centerpiece in a large bed. After leaf-fall in the autumn, catkins can be seen hanging from branches. These will bear next year's flowers. It will be necessary to plant 2 or more of different cultivars, because oddly, filberts do not accept their own pollen.

The native hickory has a prominent place in American history. It grows strong and straight. Andrew Jackson was so tough a general that his soldiers nicknamed him "Old Hickory." And many of the fence rails that Abe Lincoln split, it is believed, were of hickory.

Shagbark hickory (*Carya ovata*) and shellbark (*C. Laciniosa*) develop into splendid shade trees. They both have characteristically shaggy bark that looks like strips are peeling off which offers an interesting texture to the winter landscape. They are long-lived trees and self-pollinating. They are also known to be difficult to establish, so the nurseryman's instructions should be followed exactly if you wish to achieve success. You will be convinced to grow hickories once you have tasted the flavor of the nuts. It is similar to black walnut, but more delicate in flavor. Add them to cereal, granola or cookies. They are difficult to crack open and may take a gear-action nutcracker. My husband uses his bench vise.

Alas, the American chestnut (*Castanea dentata*) has disappeared from the countryside, but a very adequate replacement is the Chinese chestnut (*C. Mollissima*). It bears satin-smooth, sweet nuts in bristly husks that have sharp spines. The nuts fall free of the husk when they drop and should be collected promptly. A single tree will bear nuts, but not nearly as many as two or more which provide better pollination. They will mature to be fine, spreading trees, and commonly produce more than 100 pounds of nuts. A good method of cooking is to nick the shell of each nut, rinse in water, then roast in a shallow pan at 350 degrees for 30 minutes. They come out perfect.

If you never thought of starting nut trees, now is a good time to consider this option and prepare for a spring planting.

> *Many basket weavers color their reed baskets with nut stains. Acorns, black walnuts, hickory nuts and chestnuts can be stored in an ammonia solution for staining. Acorn, chestnut and hickory impart soft, blond shadings, while black walnut yields a deeper shade of brown.*

Mistletoe

Although American mistletoe (*Phoradendron serotinum*) is enjoyed as a December holiday ornamentation (for those who like to kiss or be kissed), there is not much good that can be said about it.

It is a parasite which attaches itself to the bark of deciduous trees usually being found from New Jersey to Florida and westward to Texas. If it is removed promptly upon sighting, perhaps it had not had time to penetrate the bark of its host tree yet. If it already pierces the bark, sending its roots into the host tree, it can be cut off , but will continue to grow.

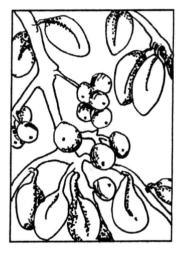

The United States Food and Drug Administration has listed this plant as "unsafe," despite early medical claims that it was used as a sedative and antihypertensive.

If your house will be decorated with some cuttings of mistletoe, be aware that berries are toxic. Care should be taken when using mistletoe around food or children.

A long time ago, in a variety store, I found a sprig of imitation mistletoe that was made of flexible plastic. It looked very real. The berries were huge and plump and leaves sort of velvety. I used it for years to hang in doorways, and it brought much merriment. If it is possible that you could find the same type of imitation, there would be no fear of the genuine plant contaminating anything or anyone, and your guests may still fulfil the urge to kiss someone who is standing under it.

Winter Visions

December brings the year's gardening cycle to a close, only to start over again as the new year enters. We will soon see the days slowly lengthening and the sun becoming stronger, albeit through ice and snow crystals. The garden catalogs are colorful and tantalizing. It is time to think, plan and dream of the ideal garden that we will have next year.

Can't you just feel your green thumb vibrating with strength?

I plan to start my seeds on time; not too late and definitely not too early. Every one of my seeds will germinate, and I'll have lots of room for everything that I ever wanted to grow -- lots of tomatoes and peppers, and room for sweet corn, pumpkins and watermelons. I'll have the most stately foxgloves, and my roses will be fit for royalty.

I'll have a bushel of green peas in June and my pole beans will climb up to the sky.

I will not permit one noxious weed to appear in my garden. If any should sneak in, they will cower when they see me coming.

The bad bugs will be routed by all the good bugs that I have invited.

We will have rain, just enough, every other night, between the hours of 2:00 and 4:00.

My neighbors will covet my 15-inch carrots and 3-pound tomatoes, but I will be generous and share with them.

I'll prepare myself for new varieties for next year, and I will try them all.

I've grown some very good gardens in the past, but this one will be the best. That's because it is the only one I can grow in the middle of December.

APPENDIX

Glossary

Annuals -- Plants that complete their life-cycle in one year's time, going from seed, to flowering, to seeds, then dying .

Half-Hardy Annual -- An annual that is raised indoors from seed, then, after being hardened off, is planted outdoors (tomato).

Hardy Annual -- An annual that is direct-seeded into the ground and completes its life cycle outdoors the same year (radish).

Arboretum -- A place where trees, shrubs & plants are grown for scientific & educational purposes.

Biennials -- Plants that take two years to grow from seed and produce flowers , then die. (Forget-me-not, fox glove).

Bract -- Leaves often located outside the small, clustered blossom of the plant itself, looking like flower petals but actually are leaves of the plant. Examples are the red of poinsettias, the white bract surrounding the flower of the peace lily (*Spathiphyllum*), and dogwoods.

BT (*Bacillus thuringiensis*) -- is a bacterium that controls plant pests. It kills the insect larvae that eat it but is harmless to humans, pets and plants. But it may kill larvae of beneficial insects.

BTK (*B. Thuringiensis* var. *kurstaki*) -- A BT product that kills common caterpillars such as tomato hornworms, cabbageworms, cabbage loopers. It is non-toxic to humans, pets and plants. Judicious use of it is recommended for specific pest larvae because it can also kill butterfly larvae. Handpicking of insects is the preferred method to use if at all possible.

Calex, or Calyx -- is the green cup that holds the petals of a flower at the top of the stem.

Composite -- (or Compositae) is a large class of flowers with many petals (daisy, dandelion, asters) the center of the "blossom" is actually the flowerhead or eye, surrounded by many petals. These are known as ray flowers.

Compost -- A mixture of organic materials assembled in a way to promote decaying for the finished product of compost which acts as a soil conditioner.

Corm -- A solid, bulb-like, underground stem, resembling a bulb, but without the layers or scales of, say, an onion. Examples are corms of crocus, gladiolus.

Cultivar -- a variety of plant that is raised by selective breeding.

Damp off -- Overwatering seedlings along with poor air circulation promotes a mildew growth that causes young plants to keel over and die.

Deadheading -- The removal of spent blossoms to prevent seed formation, directing the plant's growing energy to the roots instead of to seed production.

Deciduous -- A plant (tree or shrub) that drops its leaves in the autumn and grows new ones in the spring; not evergreen.

Determinate/Indeterminate -- In referring to tomato-growing, the determinate plants will grow to produce one crop only, often used by commercial canneries. Indeterminate varieties are those that will continue to produce fruits until frost kills the plant, making this type the most desirable for the home gardener.

Dioecious/Monoecious -- These are terms refering to reproductive habits of some plants. Simply put, dioecious are those that require a male plant plus a female plant to produce fruits or berries (hollies, persimmons). Monoecious plants are those that produce both male and female flowers on the same plant (cucumber, corn).

Direct-seeding -- planting seeds directly into the ground without having to start them indoors first.

Floribunda -- Referring to roses, the floribunda produces blooms in clusters, but each bloom is as large as a tea rose bloom.

Genus -- the first word of a plant's botanical name, always capitalized.

Grandiflora -- A term for a plant that contains both single-borne flowers and clusters, as well.

Harden off -- In growing seedlings, this is part of the process of adapting tender seedlings to the great outdoors. Keeping them outdoors in a protected area away from hot sun, strong winds or cold for a week or two will prepare them for the rigors of the garden bed. This is when watering is cut back a bit to complete the hardening-off process.

Heirloom -- These are flowers and vegetables of time-tested varieties. Their "roots" are of early European ancestry and have been passed down for generations. Flavor, hardiness and stamina have made them popular favorites. Heirloom seeds can be saved and planted each year to produce a carbon-copy plant.

Humus -- A product that comes from the breaking down, decomposing of leaves or organic debris, as would be found on a forest floor.

Hybrid -- When a plant is produced by the crossing of two genetically different parents, the first generation is called hybrid. They have obvious advantages such as vigorous growth and disease resistance. Seeds from hybrids will not reproduce to make the same plant. Growing only hybrids makes you, as a customer, rely on seed companies for future crops.

Insecticidal Soap -- A biodegradable product that kills many insects on contact without harming plants, pets, people or beneficial insects.

Invasive -- A plant with very vigorous growing habits, either by underground rhizomes, stolons or seeds, displacing less vigorous species, usually taking over wide areas. (See *Invasives*, Appendix.)

Mantid -- and praying mantid are other names for the praying mantis, a beneficial insect.

Mulch -- A layer 2, 3 or 4 inches deep of organic material used to keep garden soil moist and cool, control weeds, enrich the soil, and to prevent erosion or unsightly mud splashes on plants.

Multiflora -- A plant that produces small flowers in clusters.

Organic (material) -- That which comes from growing plants of all types; not any animal products.

Perennial -- A plant which lives for several years as opposed to annual which completes its life cycle in only one year. Perennials could include shrubs or trees.

Tender Perennial -- is a plant that while it can thrive outdoors in summer, is sensitive to cold winter temperatures and must be brought in to survive.

pH -- A measure of alkalinity and acidity of soil, developed on a scale of 1 to 14, with 7 representing neutral. Most plants grow best in a soil pH of between 6.5 and 7. An acid soil would read below 7; an alkaline soil would read above 7.

Rhizome -- Commonly refers to the underground, horizontal stems or rootstock of a plant (iris) that is more or less enlarged and elongated and is commonly misnamed root. It contains eyes (buds) for next season's growth and roots for nourishing the plant.

Side Dressing -- This is simply applying fertilizer or nutrients to the soil by spreading it onto the soil surface above the plant's root area, but keeping it directly away from the stem or trunk.

Stigma -- The part of a flower (female) that receives the pollen.

Stolons -- A branch or stem of a plant that creeps horizontally above ground and roots to produce a new plant.

Succulent -- A plant having thick, fleshy stems or leaves that store water, allowing it to live in desert-like conditions. (Jade plant, aloe.)

Tilth -- A condition of the soil that permits it to hold air and water in good balance, breaking easily into crumbs. It is loose, allowing for free root growth, and is rich in organic material.

Toxic -- poisonous, either by ingesting, or in some way irritating to the skin by touching.

Tuber -- A fleshy underground stem (potato) or root (dahlia) which permits the plant to perpetuate itself.

Pennsylvania State
Cooperative Extension Offices

Adams County, 717-334-6271
Allegheny County, 412-473-2540
Armstrong County, 724-548-3447
Beaver County, 724-774-3003
Bedford County, 814-623-4800
Berks County, 610-378-1327
Blair County, 814-940-5989
Bradford County, 570-265-2896
Bucks County, 215-345-3283
Butler County, 724-287-4761
Cambria County, 814-472-7986
Cameron County, 814-486-3350
Carbon County, 570-325-2788
Center County, 814-355-4897
Chester County, 610-696-3500
Clarion County, 814-782-0033
Clearfield County, 814-765-7878
Clinton County, 570-726-0022
Columbia County, 570-784-6660
Crawford County, 814-333-7460
Cumberland County, 717-240-6500
Dauphin County, 717-921-8803
Delaware County, 610-690-2655
Elk County, 814-776-5331
Erie County, 814-825-0900
Fayette County, 724-438-0111
Forest County, 814-755-3544
Franklin County, 717-263-9226
Fulton County, 717-485-4111
Greene County, 724-627-3745
Huntingdon County, 814-643-1660
Indiana County, 724-465-3880
Jefferson County, 814-849-7361

Pennsylvania State Cooperative Extension Offices, Contd.
Juniata County, 717-436-7744
Lackawanna County, 570-963-4761
Lancaster County, 717-394-6851
Lawrence County, 724-654-8370
Lebanon County, 717-270-4391
Lehigh County, 610-391-9840
Luzerne County, 570-825-1701
Lycoming County, 570-433-3040
McKean County, 814-887-5613
Mercer County, 724-662-3141
Mifflin County, 717-248-9618
Monroe County, 570-421-6430
Montgomery County, 610-489-4315
Montour County 570-275-3731
Northamptom County, 610-746-1970
Northumberland County, 570-988-3950
Perry County, 717-582-5150
Philadelphia County, 215-471-2200
Pike County, 570-296-3400
Potter County, 814-274-8540
Schuylkill County, 570-622-4225
Snyder County, 570-837-4252
Somerset County, 814-445-8911
Sullivan County, 570-928-8941
Susquehanna County, 570-278-1158
Tioga County, 570-724-9120
Union County, 570-524-8721
Venango County, 814-437-7607
Warren County, 814-563-9388
Washington County, 724-228-6881
Wayne County, 570-253-5970
Westmoreland County, 724-837-1402
Wyoming County, 570-836-3196
York County, 717-840-7408

In New Jersey

Extension Office telephone numbers for counties in the State of New Jersey can be obtained by calling Rutgers Cooperative Extension at 908-932-9306.

Invasive Plants

As explained in the Glossary, an invasive plant is one that has become a pest or weed, spreading itself by way of seed, stolons or rhizomes, overtaking other, less aggressive species. They are usually unsuitable because they are difficult to control. Most invasives are alien, or non-native, but a few are indiginous to this area. The invasives are a main reason for the decline of native plants. Some plants are known to be invasive but are still able to be purchased from nurseries or greenhouses. Even when cultivated in your own yard, these may escape to the landscape at large and become a problem for years to come. Listed below are those that the State of Pennsylvania deems invasive and to be avoided or destroyed, and are seen with increasing frequency in the southeastern section of the state.

Common Name	Botanical Name
Garlic mustard	Allaria petiolata
Musk thistle	Carduus nutans
Canada thistle	Cirsium arvense
Bull thistle	Cirsium vulgare
Jimson weed	Datura stramonium
Purple loosestrife	Lythrum alatum
Japanese stilt grass	Microstegium vinimeum
Common reed	Phragmites australis
Japanese knotweed	Polygonum cuspidatum
Shattercane	Sorghum bicolor
Johnson grass	Sorghum halepense
Autumn olive	Elaeagnus umbellata
Amur honeysuckle	Lonicera maackii

Morrow's honeysuckle	Lonicera morrowii
Standish honeysuckle	Lonicera standishii
Tartarian honeysuckle	Lonicera tatarica
Multiflora rose	Rosa multiflora
Norway Maple	Acer platanoides
Tree-of-Heaven	Ailanthus altissima
Oriental bittersweet	Celastrus orbiculatus
Japanese honeysuckle	Lonicera japonica
Mile-a-minute vine	Polygonum perfoliatum
Kudzu	Peuraria lobata
Goutweed	Aegopodium podagraria
Cheatgrass	Bromus tectorum
Dame's Rocket	Hesperis matronalis
Star of Bethlehem	Ornithogallum nutans
Wild parsnip	Pastinaca sativa
Beefsteak plant	Perilla frutenscens
Japanese barberry	Berberis thunbergii
European barberry	Berberis vulgaris
Privet	Ligustrum
Common buckthorn	Rhamnus catharticus
Wineberry	Rubus phoenicolasius
Porcelain berry	Ampelopsis brevipedunculata
Crown vetch	Coronilla varia
Day lily	Hemerocallis fulva
Cocklebur	Xanthium spp.
English ivy	Hedera helix
Periwinkle	Vinca minor
Wisteria	Wisteria floribunda
Russian olive	Elegnus angustifolium
Autumn olive	Elegnus umbellata
Catalpa	catalpa sp.
White mulberry	Morus alba
Empress tree	Paulownia tomentosa
Ajuga, bugle weed	Ajuga reptans

Plants Deer Commonly Eat and Those They Avoid

Overpopulation of deer causes much frustration among gardeners. Before we came along and grew things in our gardens, deer foraged on their own on what nature provided. However, we make it easier for them by adding such tasty morsels as hosta and rhododendrons to the landscape. The lists below may be helpful, but bear in mind, that if the deer herd is large, if it has been a bad winter, or if your property lies on a traditional deer path, there is little hope. When hungry, they will eat almost anything, except (I have found) plants that are hairy or stickery, have a strong smell or those plants with a milky, sometimes toxic, sap. Many of the plants that are listed below as "deer resistant" are natives. It may be a good idea to include many native varieties in your gardens.

Deer are known to eat:	Plants that are less foraged by deer:
Aster	
Azalea	Adonis
Campanulas	Allium
Crocus	Alyssum
Trout lily	Amsonia/Blue star
Fuchsia	Artemesia
Ivy	Aster
Helleborus (lenten rose)	Astilbe
Day lily	Aucuba
Hosta	Barrenwort
Holly	Begonia
Iris	Bergenia
Lilies	Black-eyed susans
Lobelia	Bleeding heart
Penstemons	Boxwood
Rhododendrons	Buddleia
Tulips	Butterfly weed
Violets	Clematis

Columbine
Comfrey
Coral bells
Coreopsis
Cotoneaster
Cyclamen
Daffodils
Delphinium
Deutsia
Echinacea/coneflower
Ferns
Forsythia
Fox Glove
Fritillaria
Geranium, wild
Goldenrods
Hens & chicks
Hepatica
Hibiscus
Hydrangea
Jack-in-the-pulpit
Jacob's ladder
Lady's Mantle
Lamium
Lantana
Lilac
Lily of the valley
Lunaria/Money plant
Lungwort
Magnolia

Milkweed
Mints
Monarda
Nigella
Pachysandra
Phlox
Pieris Japonica
Peony
Potentilla
Primrose
Pyracantha
Ranunculus
Redbud tree
Rose, rugosa
Rosemary
Salvias
Sedum
Snowberry
Snow-in-summer
Snow drops
Spirea
Valerian
Verbena
Viburnums
Virginia Blue bells
Veronica
Weigela
Witch hazel tree
Yarrow
Yucca

About the Author

JEAN SKEATH STAHL became a gardener and a writer early in life. After 1989, as her newspaper garden columns gained momentum, she became interested in other aspects of the outdoors as well, writing many nature and garden articles for local newsletters.

Jean is a Montgomery County, PA, Master Gardener and a winner of a 2001 Press Award given by the Pennsylvania Newspaper Association. She appears bi-monthly on WNPV radio, Lansdale PA, for a garden talk show. She is a member of the Garden Writers Association of America and past chairman of the Goschenhoppen Historians' Folk Festival Garden. Also for the Goschenhoppen Historians, she is their monthly newsletter editor. Her gardens at home are certified by the National Wildlife Federation as a Natural Wildlife Habitat.

Jean and her husband Ray live on 17 acres of woodland in southeastern Pennsylvania, where they carved into the forest a half-acre clearing. In this clearing has been Jean's garden, in which she has grown her vegetables, flowers and herbs. She has created gardens and a fish pond near the house as well.

Order Form

Now that you have read THE GARDEN LOG, would you like to order copies for friends? Complete the form below, enclose a check for the entire amount, payable to JEAN SKEATH STAHL. Include your telephone number. Mail to

Jean Stahl's Garden Log
P.O.Box 500
Tylersport, PA 18971

Telephone: 215-234-8108   FAX: 215-234-8464
(Listen for instructions)

Visit my website: www.thegardenlog.com

-----✂------------------------✂------------------------✂-----

Please send me _____ copies of *The Garden Log.*

☐ Yes, I would like each book AUTOGRAPHED by the author.

☐ Yes, I would like a FREE GIFT BOOKMARK with each book.

Quantity	Price Each	Total Price
	$17.00	$_____

Add $3.50 shipping and handling per book $_____
                                        Total Cost $_____
Pennsylvania residents add 6% Sales Tax $_____
Total amount of order: $_____

Print Clearly

Name _____

Address _____

City, State, Zip _____

Telephone Number _____

Email address _____